Cummings

Rick Steves®

SNAPSHOT

Stockholm

Cummings

CONTENTS

INTRODUCTION

This Snapshot guide, excerpted from my guidebook *Rick Steves Scandinavia*, introduces you to Stockholm, the bustling capital of Sweden. With its modern buildings and dedication to green living, Stockholm has the feel of a gleaming metropolis, but it offers a satisfying blend of Old World charm and 21st-century tech. Start at its core with a stroll through the Old Town, Gamla Stan. Then visit the *Vasa* Museum with its 17th-century warship, the Nordic Museum covering five centuries of Swedish lifestyles, and Europe's original—and unsurpassed—open-air folk museum, Skansen. Indulge yourself in this city's aristocratic delights, including the Changing of the Guard at the Royal Palace and the elaborate *smörgåsbord* at the Grand Hotel. For a side-trip, visit Drottningholm Palace, the royal family's opulent summer get-away, or Uppsala, a classic university town with a soaring cathedral. Then catch a boat and unwind among Sweden's rocky garden of more than 30,000 islands—Stockholm's Archipelago. Here in Stockholm's playground, you can count the pretty red cottages, go for a lazy stroll or bike ride, or relax on a sandy beach.

To help you have the best trip possible, I've included the following topics in this book:

• **Planning Your Time,** with advice on how to make the most of your limited time

• **Orientation,** including tourist information (abbreviated as TI), tips on public transportation, local tour options, and helpful hints

• **Sights** with ratings:

▲▲▲—Don't miss

▲▲—Try hard to see

▲—Worthwhile if you can make it

No rating—Worth knowing about

- **Sleeping** and **Eating,** with good-value recommendations in every price range
- **Connections,** with tips on trains, buses, boats, and driving
Practicalities, near the end of this book, has information on money, phoning, hotel reservations, transportation, and more.

To travel smartly, read this little book in its entirety before you go. It's my hope that this guide will make your trip more meaningful and rewarding. Traveling like a temporary local, you'll get the absolute most out of every mile, minute, and dollar.

Ha en bra resa! Happy travels!

Rick Steves

SWEDEN

SWEDEN

Sverige

Scandinavia's heartland, Sweden is far bigger than Denmark and far flatter than Norway. This family-friendly land is home to Ikea, Volvo, WikiLeaks, ABBA, and long summer vacations at red-painted, white-trimmed summer cottages. Its capital, Stockholm, is Scandinavia's grandest city.

Once the capital of blond, Sweden is now home to a growing immigrant population. Sweden is committed to its peoples' safety and security, and proud of its success in creating a society with one of the lowest poverty rates in the world. Yet Sweden has thrown in its lot with the European Union, and locals debate whether to open their economy even further.

Swedes are often stereotyped as sex-crazed, which could not be further from the truth. Several steamy films and film stars from the 1950s and 1960s stuck Sweden with the sexpot stereotype, which still reverberates among male tourists. Italians continue to travel up to Sweden looking for those bra-less, loose, and lascivious blondes...but the real story is that Sweden simply relaxed film cen-

sorship earlier than other European countries. The Swedish newspaper ad at right shows typical stereotypes, and asks, "Do you see the world as the world sees you?" Like other Scandinavians, Swedes are frank and open about sexuality. Sex education in schools is routine, living together before marriage is the norm (and has been common for centuries), and teenagers have easy access to condoms. But Swedes, who are the most unmarried people in the world, choose their partners carefully.

Before the year 2000, Sweden was a Lutheran state, with the Church of Sweden as its official religion. Until 1996, Swedes automatically became members of the Lutheran Church at birth if one parent was Lutheran. Now you need to choose to join the church, and although the culture is nominally Lutheran, few people attend services regularly. While church is handy for Christmas, Easter,

marriages, and burials, most Swedes are more likely to find religion in nature, hiking in the vast forests or fishing in one of the thousands of lakes or rivers.

Sweden is almost 80 percent wilderness, and modern legislation incorporates an ancient common law called *allemans rätt*, which guarantees people the right to move freely through Sweden's natural scenery without asking landowners for permission, as long as they behave responsibly. In summer, Swedes take advantage of the long days and warm evenings for festivals such as Midsummer (in late June) and for crayfish parties in August. Many Swedes have a summer cottage—or know someone who has one—where they spend countless hours swimming, soaking up the sun, and devouring boxes of juicy strawberries.

While Denmark and Norway look westward to Britain and the Atlantic, Sweden has always faced east, across the Baltic Sea. As Vikings, Norwegians went west to Iceland, Greenland, and

Sweden Almanac

Official Name: Konungariket Sverige—the Kingdom of Sweden—or simply Sweden.

Population: Sweden's 9.7 million people (about 56 per square mile) are mostly ethnically Swedish. Foreign-born and first-generation immigrants account for about 15 percent of the population and are primarily from Finland, the former Yugoslavia, and the Middle East. Sweden is also home to about 20,000 indigenous Sami people. Swedish is the dominant language, with most speaking English as well. While immigrants bring their various religions with them, ethnic Swedes who go to church tend to be Lutheran. For great electronic fact sheets on everything in Swedish society from religion to the Sami people, see www.sweden.se.

Latitude and Longitude: 62°N and 15°E, similar latitude to Canada's Northwest Territories.

Area: 174,000 square miles (a little bigger than California).

Geography: A chain of mountains divides Sweden from Norway on the Scandinavian Peninsula. Sweden's mostly forested landscape is flanked to the east by the Baltic Sea, which contributes to the temperate climate. Sweden also encompasses several islands, of which Gotland and Öland are the largest.

Biggest City: Sweden's capital city, Stockholm, has a population of 897,000, with more than two million in the metropolitan area. Göteborg (526,000) and Malmö (307,000) are the next-largest cities.

Economy: Sweden has a $394 billion Gross Domestic Product and a per capita GDP of $40,900—similar to Canada's. Manufacturing, telecommunications, automobiles, and pharmaceuticals rank among its top industries, along with timber, hydropower, and iron ore. The Swedish economy emerged

America; Danes headed south to England, France, and the Mediterranean; and Swedes went east into Russia. (The word "Russia" has Viking roots.) In the early Middle Ages, Swedes founded the Russian cities of Nizhny Novgorod and Kiev, and even served as royal guards in Constantinople (modern-day Istanbul). During the later Middle Ages, German settlers and traders strongly  influenced Sweden's culture and language. By the 17th century, Sweden was a major European power, with one of the largest naval fleets in Europe and an empire extending around the Baltic, including Finland, Estonia, Latvia, and parts of Poland, Russia, and

from the recent financial crisis as one of the strongest in Europe, helped by its competitive high-tech businesses—and by the government's generally conservative fiscal policies. Eighty percent of Swedish workers belong to a labor union.

Currency: 7 Swedish kronor (kr, officially SEK) = about $1.

Government: King Carl XVI Gustav is the ceremonial head of Sweden's constitutional monarchy. Elected every four years, the 349-member Swedish Parliament (Riksdag) is currently led by Prime Minister Stefan Löfven of the Social Democratic Party (elected in October 2014). *The Economist* magazine—which considered factors such as participation, impact of people on their government, and transparency—ranked Sweden by far the world's most democratic country (followed by the other Scandinavian countries and the Netherlands, with North Korea coming in last).

Flag: The Swedish flag is blue with a yellow Scandinavian cross. The colors are derived from the Swedish coat of arms, with yellow symbolizing the generosity of the people and blue representing vigilance, truth, loyalty, perseverance, and justice.

The Average Swede: He or she is 41 years old, has 1.88 children, and will live to be 82.

Germany. But by the early 19th century, Sweden's war-weary empire had shrunk. The country's current borders date from 1809.

During a massive wave of emigration from the 1860s to World War II, about a quarter of Sweden's people left for the Promised Land—America. Many emigrants were farmers from the southern region of Småland. The House of Emigrants museum in Växjö tells their story, as do the movies *The Emigrants* and *The New Land*, based on the series of books by Vilhelm Moberg.

The 20th century was good to Sweden. While other European countries were embroiled in the two World Wars, neutral Sweden grew stronger, finding a balance between the extremes of communism and the free market. After a recession hit in the early 1990s, and the collapse of Soviet communism reshaped the European political scene, some started to criticize Sweden's "middle way" as extreme and unworkable. But during the late 1990s and early 2000s,

Sweden's economy improved, buoyed by a strong lineup of successful multinational companies. Volvo, Scania (trucks and machinery), Ikea, and Ericsson (the telecommunications giant) are leading the way in manufacturing, design, and technology.

The 2008-2009 economic downturn, however, had its impact on Sweden's export-driven economy—its Saab car manufacturer filed for bankruptcy protection in 2011. Unemployment has ticked upward (although it remains enviably low compared to other countries), and Sweden's famously generous welfare systems are feeling the pressure. Although things have rebounded since the crisis, the country's fortunes are dogged by the overall economic weakness of the European Union—Sweden's main export market.

Sweden has come a long way when it comes to accepting immigrants. Less than a century ago, only Swedes who traveled overseas were likely to ever see people of different ethnicities. In 1927 a black man worked in a Stockholm gas station, and people journeyed from great distances to fill up their car there... just to get a look. (Business boomed and his job was secure.)

Since the 1960s, however, Sweden (like Denmark and Norway) has accepted many immigrants and refugees from southeastern Europe, the Middle East, and elsewhere. This praiseworthy humanitarian policy has dramatically—and sometimes painfully—diversified a formerly homogenous country. Many of the service-industry workers you will meet have come to Sweden from elsewhere.

More recently, with refugees flooding in from Syria and Iraq, Swedish social services have been tested as never before. The politics of immigration have become more complex and intense, as Swedes debate the costs (real and societal) of maintaining a culture that wants to be blind to class differences and ethnic divisions.

Though most Swedes speak English, and communication is rarely an issue, a few Swedish words are helpful and appreciated. "Hello" is *"Hej"* (hey) and "Good-bye" is *"Hej då"* (hey doh). "Thank you" is *"Tack"* (tack), which can also double for "please." For a longer list of Swedish survival phrases, see the following page.

Swedish Survival Phrases

Swedish pronunciation (especially the vowel sounds) can be tricky for Americans to say, and there's quite a bit of variation across the country; listen closely to locals and imitate, or ask for help. The most difficult Swedish sound is *sj*, which sounds roughly like a guttural "*h*w" (made in your throat); however, like many sounds, this is pronounced differently in various regions—for example, Stockholmers might say it more like "shw."

English	Swedish	Pronunciation
Hello. (formal)	Goddag!	goh-**dah**
Hi. / Bye. (informal)	Hej. / Hej då.	hey / hey doh
Do you speak English?	Talar du engelska?	**tah**-lar doo **eng**-ehl-skah
Yes. / No.	Ja. / Nej.	yaw / nay
Please.	Snälla. / Tack.*	**snehl**-lah / tack
Thank you (very much).	Tack (så mycket).	tack (soh **mee**-keh)
You're welcome.	Ingen orsak.	**eeng**-ehn **oor**-sahk
Can I help you?	Kan jag hjälpa dig?	kahn yaw **jehl**-pah day
Excuse me.	Ursäkta.	**oor**-sehk-tah
(Very) good.	(Mycket) bra.	(**mee**-keh) brah
Goodbye.	Adjö.	ah-**yew**
one / two	en / två	ehn / tvoh
three / four	tre / fyra	treh / **fee**-rah
five / six	fem / sex	fehm / sehks
seven / eight	sju / åtta	*h*woo / **oh**-tah
nine / ten	nio / tio	**nee**-oh / **tee**-oh
hundred	hundra	**hoon**-drah
thousand	tusen	**too**-sehn
How much?	Hur mycket?	hewr **mee**-keh
local currency: (Swedish) kronor	(Svenske) kronor	(svehn-**skeh**) **kroh**-nor
Where is...?	Var finns...?	var feens
...the toilet	...toaletten	toh-ah-**leh**-tehn
men	man	mahn
women	kvinna	**kvee**-nah
water / coffee	vatten / kaffe	**vah**-tehn / **kah**-feh
beer / wine	öl / vin	url / veen
Cheers!	Skål!	skohl
The bill, please.	Kan jag få notan, tack.	kahn yaw foh **noh**-tahn tack

*Swedish has various ways to say "please," depending on the context. The simplest is *snälla,* but Swedes sometimes use the word *tack* (thank you) the way we use "please."

STOCKHOLM

If I had to call one European city home, it might be Stockholm. One-third water, one-third parks, one-third city, on the sea, surrounded by woods, bubbling with energy and history, Sweden's stunning capital is green, clean, and underrated.

The city is built on a string of islands connected by bridges. Its location midway along the Baltic Sea, behind the natural fortification of its archipelago, made it a fine port, vital to the economy and security of the Swedish peninsula. In the 1500s, Stockholm became a political center when Gustav Vasa established the monarchy (1523). A century later, the expansionist King Gustavus Adolphus made it an influential European capital. The Industrial Revolution brought factories and a flood of farmers from the countryside. In the 20th century, the fuming smokestacks were replaced with steel-and-glass Modernist buildings housing high-tech workers and an expanding service sector.

Today, with more than two million people in the greater metropolitan area (one in five Swedes), Stockholm is Sweden's largest city, as well as its cultural, educational, and media center. It's also the country's most ethnically diverse city. Despite its size, Stockholm is committed to limiting its environmental footprint. Development is strictly monitored, and pollution-belching cars must pay a toll to enter the city. If there's a downside to Stockholm, it's that the city feels super-wealthy (even its Mac-toting hipsters), sometimes snobby, and a bit sure of itself. Stockholm rivals Oslo in expense, and beats it in pretense.

For the visitor, Stockholm offers both old and new. Crawl through Europe's best-preserved old warship and relax on a scenic harbor boat tour. Browse the cobbles and antique shops of the lantern-lit Old Town. Take a trip back in time at Skansen, Europe's first and best open-air folk museum. Marvel at Stockholm's glittering City Hall, slick shopping malls, and art museums. (Even "also ran" museums in this city rank high on the European scale.) Explore the funky vibrancy of the hipster/foodie/design-forward Södermalm district.

While progressive and sleek, Stockholm respects its heritage. In summer, military bands parade daily through the heart of town to the Royal Palace, announcing the Changing of the Guard and turning even the most dignified tourist into a scampering kid.

With extra time, travelers can consider several Stockholm side-trips, including the nearby royal residence, Drottningholm Palace; the cute town of Sigtuna; or the university town of Uppsala, with its grand cathedral and Iron Age mounds (see the Near Stockholm chapter). Stockholm is also an ideal home base for cruising to island destinations in the city's archipelago (see Stockholm's Archipelago chapter).

PLANNING YOUR TIME

On a two- to three-week trip through Scandinavia, Stockholm is worth two days. For the busiest and best two- to three-day plan, I'd suggest this:

Day 1: 10:00—See the *Vasa* warship (movie and tour); 12:00—Visit the Nordic Museum; 13:30—Tour the Skansen open-air museum and grab lunch there; 16:00—Ride the boat (or tram #7) to Nybroplan and follow my self-guided walk through the modern city from  Kungsträdgården; 18:30—Take the Royal Canal boat tour (confirm last sailing time, no boats Jan-March).

Day 2: 10:00—Ride one of the city orientation bus tours (either the hop-on, hop-off or the 1.25-hour bus tour from the Royal Opera House), or take the City Hall tour and climb its tower; 12:15—Catch the Changing of the Guard at the palace (13:15 on Sun); 13:00—Lunch on Stortorget; 14:00—Tour the Royal Armory (and, if time and budget allow, the Nobel Museum and/or Royal Palace sights), and follow my Old Town self-guided walk; 18:30—Explore Södermalm for dinner—it's just across the locks from Gamla Stan—or take a harbor dinner cruise.

Day 3: With an extra day, add a cruise through the scenic island archipelago (easy to do from Stockholm), visit the royal palace at Drottningholm, take a side-trip to charming Sigtuna or Up-

psala, or spend more time in Stockholm (there's plenty left to do and experience).

Orientation to Stockholm

Greater Stockholm's two million residents live on 14 islands woven together by 54 bridges. Visitors need only concern themselves with these districts, most of which are islands:

Norrmalm is downtown, with most of the hotels and shopping areas, and the combined train and bus station. **Östermalm,** to the east, is more residential.

Kungsholmen, the mostly suburban island across from Norrmalm, is home to City Hall and inviting lakefront eateries.

Gamla Stan is the Old Town island of winding, lantern-lit streets, antiques shops, and classy cafés clustered around the Royal Palace. The adjacent **Riddarholmen** is similarly atmospheric, but much sleepier. The locks between Lake Mälaren (to the west) and the Baltic Sea (to the east) are at a junction called **Slussen,** just south of Gamla Stan on the way to Södermalm.

Skeppsholmen is the small, central, traffic-free park/island with the Museum of Modern Art and two fine youth hostels.

Djurgården is the park-island—Stockholm's wonderful green playground, with many of the city's top sights (bike rentals just over bridge as you enter island).

Södermalm, just south of the other districts, is sometimes called "Stockholm's Brooklyn"—young, creative, and trendy. Apart from its fine views and some good eateries, this residential island may be of less interest to those on a quick visit.

TOURIST INFORMATION

Stockholm has two TI organizations, one far better than the other. The helpful city-run TI—called **Visit Stockholm**—has two branches. The main office is downtown in the Kulturhuset, facing Sergels Torg (Mon-Fri 9:00-19:00—until 18:00 off-season, Sat 9:00-16:00, Sun 10:00-16:00, Sergels Torg 3, T-bana: T-Centralen, tel. 08/5082-8508, www.visitstockholm.com). They also have a branch at the airport, in Terminal 5, where most international flights arrive (long hours daily, tel. 08/797-6000). The efficient staff provides free city maps, the glossy *Stockholm Guide* booklet that introduces the city, the monthly *What's On* leaflet, Stockholm Cards (described later), transportation passes, day-trip and bus-tour information and tickets, and a room-booking service (small fee). Take a number as you enter, or avoid the wait by looking up sightseeing details on one of the user-friendly computer terminals (they can also give you the code for free Wi-Fi).

Around town, you'll also see the green *i* logo of the other "tourist information" service, **Stockholm Info,** run by a for-profit agency. While less helpful than the official TI, they hand out maps and brochures, sell Stockholm Cards, and may be able to answer basic questions (locations include train station's main hall, Gamla Stan, and Gallerian mall).

Stockholm Card: This 24-hour pass includes all public transit, entry to almost every sight (80 attractions), plus some free or discounted tours for 525 kr. An added bonus is the substantial pleasure of doing everything without considering the cost (many of Stockholm's sights are worth the time but not the money). The card pays for itself if you use public transportation and see Skansen, the Vasa Museum, and Drottningholm Palace. You can stretch it by entering Skansen on your 24th hour. A child's pass (age 7-17) costs about 60 percent less. The Stockholm Card also comes in 48-hour (675 kr), 72-hour (825 kr), and 120-hour (1,095 kr) versions. Cards are sold at the Visit Stockholm TIs, the unofficial Stockholm Info offices, many hotels and hostels, larger subway stations, and at www.visitstockholm.com.

ARRIVAL IN STOCKHOLM
By Train or Bus

Stockholm's adjacent train (Centralstation) and bus (Cityterminalen) stations, at the southwestern edge of Norrmalm, are a hive of services (including an unofficial Stockholm Info "TI"), eateries, shops, exchange desks, and people on the move. From the train station, the bus station is up the escalators from the main hall and through the glassy atrium (lined with sales desks for bus companies and cruise lines). Those sailing to Finland or Estonia can catch a shuttle bus to the port from the bus terminal. Underground is the T-Centralen subway (T-bana) station—probably the easiest way to reach your hotel. Taxi stands are outside. The best way to connect the city and its airport is via the Arlanda Express shuttle train, which leaves from tracks 1

and 2 (follow *Arlanda Express/airport train* signs through the station; see below).

By Plane
Arlanda Airport
Stockholm's Arlanda Airport is 28 miles north of town (airport code: ARN, tel. 08/797-6000, www.arlanda.se). The airport TI (described earlier) can advise you on getting into Stockholm and on your sightseeing plans.

Getting Between the Airport and Downtown: The **airport train,** the Arlanda Express, is the fastest way to zip between the airport and the central train station. Traveling most of the way at 125 mph, it gets you downtown in just 20 minutes—but it's not cheap (260 kr one-way, 490 kr round-trip, free for kids under age 17 with adult, covered by rail pass; generally 4/hour—departing at :05, :20, :35, and :50 past the hour in each direction; toll-free tel. 020-222-224, www.arlandaexpress.com). Buy your ticket either at the window near the track or from a ticket-vending machine, or pay an extra 100 kr to buy it on board. In summer and on weekends, a special fare lets two people travel for nearly half-price (two for 280 kr one-way, available daily mid-June-Aug, Thu-Sun year-round).

Airport shuttle buses (Flygbussarna) run between the airport and Stockholm's train/bus stations (119 kr, 6/hour, 40 minutes, may take longer at rush hour, buy tickets from station kiosks or at airport TI, www.flygbussarna.se).

Taxis between the airport and the city center take 30-40 minutes (about 520 kr, depends on company, look for price printed on side of cab). Establish the price first. Reputable taxis accept credit cards.

The **cheapest airport connection** is to take bus #583 from the airport to Märsta, then switch to the *pendeltåg* (suburban train,

4/hour), which goes to Stockholm's central train station (72 kr, 1 hour total journey time, covered by Stockholm Card).

Skavsta Airport

Some discount airlines use Skavsta Airport, about 60 miles south of Stockholm (airport code: NYO, www.skavsta.se). Flygbussarna shuttle buses connect to the city (159 kr, cheaper if you buy online in advance, about 1-2/hour—generally timed to meet arriving flights, 80 minutes, www.flygbussarna.se).

By Car

Only a Swedish meatball would drive a car in Stockholm. Park it and use public transit instead. The TI has a *Parking in Stockholm* brochure. Those sailing to Finland or Estonia should ask about long-term parking at the terminal when reserving tickets; to minimize the risk of theft and vandalism, pay extra for the most secure parking garage.

HELPFUL HINTS

Theft Alert: Even in Stockholm, when there are crowds, there are pickpockets (such as at the Royal Palace during the Changing of the Guard). Too-young-to-arrest teens—many from other countries—are hard for local police to control.

Emergency Assistance: In case of an emergency, dial 112.

Medical Help: For around-the-clock medical advice, call 1177. The **C. W. Scheele** 24-hour pharmacy is near the train station at Klarabergsgatan 64 (tel. 08/454-8130).

English Bookstore: The aptly named **English Bookshop,** in Gamla Stan, sells a variety of reading materials (including Swedish-interest books) in English (Mon-Fri 10:00-18:30, Sat 10:00-16:00, Sun 12:00-15:00, Lilla Nygatan 11, tel. 08/790-5510).

Laundry: Tvättomaten is a rare find—the only independent launderette in Stockholm (self-service-100 kr/load, 48-hour full-service-200 kr/load—bring it in early and you can get it back at the end of the day; open Mon-Fri 8:30-18:30—until 17:00 in July-mid-Aug, Sat 9:30-13:00, closed Sun; across from Gustav Vasa church, Västmannagatan 61 on Odenplan, T-bana: Odenplan, tel. 08/346-480, www.tvattomaten.com).

Updates to This Book: For updates to this book, check www.ricksteves.com/update.

GETTING AROUND STOCKHOLM
By Public Transit

Stockholm's fine but pricey public transport network (officially Storstockholms Lokaltrafik—but signed as *SL*) includes subway

(Tunnelbana, called "T-bana") and bus systems, and a single handy tram from the commercial center to the sights at Djurgården. It's a spread-out city, so most visitors will need public transport at some point (transit info tel. 08/600-1000, press * for English, www.sl.se/english). The subway is easy to figure out, but many sights are

better served by bus. The main lines are listed on the back of the official city map. A more detailed system map is posted around town and available free from subway ticket windows and SL info desks in main stations. Check out the modern public art in the subway (such as at Kungsträdgården Station).

Tickets: A single ride for subway, tram, or bus costs 36 kr (up to 1.25 hours, including transfers); a 24-hour pass is 115 kr, while a 72-hour pass is 230 kr. Tickets are sold on the tram, but not on board buses—buy one before you board.

You can choose whether to buy paper tickets or get an SL-Access fare card. **Paper tickets** are sold at the Pressbyrån newsstands scattered throughout the city, inside almost every T-bana station, and at some transit-ticket offices (all SL ticket-sellers are clearly marked with a blue flag with the *SL* logo); they are not available at self-service machines.

Locals and savvy tourists carry a blue **SL-Access card,** which you touch against the blue pad to enter the T-bana turnstile or when boarding a bus or tram. If planning to use public transit for more than a few rides, the card can save you money (200 kr for 8 rides, 20-kr deposit for card). You can top up your card at self-service machines (US credit cards work if you know your PIN). Cards are good for several years, so you can pass it along or save it for a return trip.

By Harbor Shuttle Ferry

In summer, ferries let you make a fun, practical, and scenic shortcut across the harbor to Djurgården Island. Boats leave from Slussen (at the south end of Gamla Stan), docking near the Gröna Lund amusement park on Djurgården (45 kr, covered by public-transit passes, 3-4/hour, May-mid-Sept only, 10-minute trip, tel. 08/679-5830, www.waxholmsbolaget.se). On some runs, this ferry also stops near the Museum of Modern Art on Skeppsholmen Island. The Nybro ferry makes the five-minute journey from Nybroplan to Djurgården, landing next to the Vasa Museum (55 kr, credit cards only, 1/hour, April-Sept daily roughly 9:00-18:00, tel. 08/731-0025, www.ressel.se). While buses and trams run between the same points more frequently, the ferry option gets you out onto the water and can be faster—and certainly more scenic—than overland connections. The hop-on, hop-off boat tour also connects many of these stops.

By Taxi

Stockholm is a good taxi town—provided you find a reputable cab that charges fair rates. Taxis are unregulated, so companies can charge whatever they like. Before hopping in a taxi, look carefully at the big yellow label in the back window, which lists various fares. On the left, you'll see the per-kilometer fares for weekdays, evenings and weekends, and holidays. The largest number, on the right, shows their "highest comparison price" *(högsta järnförpriset)* for a 10-kilometer ride that lasts 15 minutes; this number should be between 290 and 390—if it's higher, move on. (Legally, you're not obligated to take the first cab in line—feel free to compare fares.) Most cabs charge a drop fee of about 45 kr. Taxis with inflated rates tend to congregate at touristy places like the Vasa Museum or in Gamla Stan. I've been ripped off enough by cabs here to know: Take only "Taxi Stockholm" cabs with the phone number (08/150-000) printed on the door. (Other companies that are reportedly honest include Taxi Kurir, tel. 08/300-000, and Taxi 020, tel. 08/850-400 or 020-20-20-20.) Your hotel, restaurant, or museum can call a cab, which will generally arrive within minutes (no extra charge—the meter starts when you hop in).

Tours in Stockholm

The sightseeing company **Strömma** has a lock on most city tours, whether by bus, by boat, or on foot. Their website (www.stromma. se) covers the entire program, much of which is listed next. For more information on their tours, call 08/1200-4000. Tours can be paid for in advance online, or simply as you board. The Stockholm Card provides discounts or even covers some of Strömma's tours, including the Royal Canal or Historic Canal boat trip (free), their orientation bus tour (half-price), and their hop-on, hop-off bus tour (discounted).

BY BUS
Hop-On, Hop-Off Bus Tour
Three hop-on, hop-off buses make a 1.5-hour circuit of the city, orienting riders with a recorded commentary and linking all the essential places from Skansen to City Hall; when cruises are in town, they also stop at both cruise ports (Stadsgården and Frihamnen). **Open Top Tours'** green buses and **City Sightseeing's** red buses both cooperate with Strömma (260 kr/24 hours, 350 kr/72 hours, ticket covers both buses; May-Sept 2/hour daily 10:00-

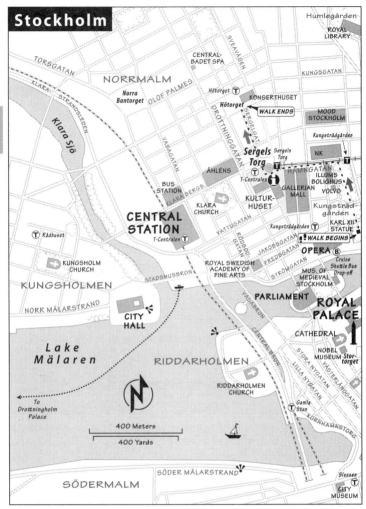

16:00, fewer off-season, none mid-Jan-mid-Feb, www.stromma. se). **Red Sightseeing** offers a similar hop-on, hop-off itinerary for the same price (3/hour, www.redbuses.se). All bus companies offer free Wi-Fi.

Quickie Orientation Bus Tour

Several different city bus tours leave from the Royal Opera House on Gustav Adolfs Torg. Strömma's Stockholm Panorama tour provides a good overview—but, as it's the same price as the 24-hour hop-on, hop-off ticket, I'd take this tour only if you want a quick and efficient loop with no unnecessary stops (260 kr, 4-6/day, fewer in Oct-May, 1.25 hours).

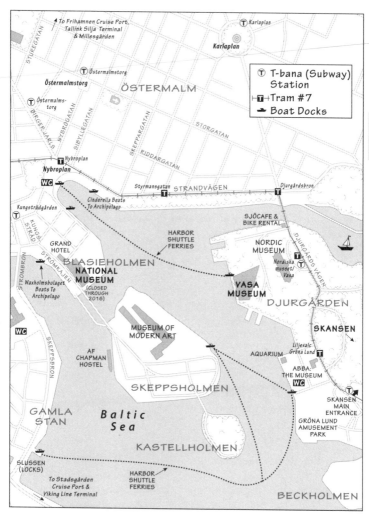

BY BOAT
▲City Boat Tours

For a good floating look at Stockholm and a pleasant break, consider a sightseeing cruise. I enjoy these various boat tours at the end of the day, when the light is warm and the sights and museums are closed. The handiest are the Strömma/ Stockholm Sightseeing boats, which leave from Strömkajen, in front of the Grand Hotel,

and also stop at Nybroplan five minutes later. The **Royal Canal Tour** is short and informative (170 kr, 50 minutes, departs at :30 past each hour May-Aug 10:30-18:30, less frequent off-season, none Jan-March). The nearly two-hour **Under the Bridges Tour** goes through two locks and under 15 bridges (225 kr, departures on the hour May-mid-Sept). The **Historic Canal Tour** leaves from the Stadshusbron dock at City Hall (170 kr, 50 minutes, departs at :30 past each hour June-Aug). You'll circle Kungsholmen island while learning about Stockholm's history from the early Industrial Age to modern times.

Hop-On, Hop-Off Boat Tour

Stockholm is a city surrounded by water, making this boat option enjoyable and practical. Strömma/Royal Sightseeing offers the same small loop, stopping at key spots such as Djurgården (Skansen and Vasa Museum), Gamla Stan (near Slussen and again near Royal Palace), the Viking Line dock next to the cruise terminal at Stadsgården, and Nybroplan. Use the boat strictly as transport from Point A to Point B, or make the whole one-hour, eight-stop loop and enjoy the recorded commentary (Strömma-160 kr/24 hours, Royal Sightseeing-120 kr/24 hours, 2-3/hour May-mid-Sept, pick up map for schedule and locations of boat stops, www.stromma.se or www.royalsightseeing.com).

ON FOOT
Old Town Walk

Strömma offers a 1.25-hour Old Town walk (150 kr, 2/day July-Aug only, departs from obelisk next to Royal Palace on Gamla Stan).

Local Guides

Håkan Frändén is an excellent guide who brings Stockholm to life (mobile 070-531-3379, hakan.franden@hotmail.com). You can also hire a private guide through the Association of Qualified Tourist Guides of Stockholm (www.guidestockholm.com, info@guidestockholm.com). The standard rate is about 1,500 kr for up to three hours. **Marita Bergman** is a teacher and a licensed guide who enjoys showing visitors around during her school breaks (1,650 kr/half-day tour, mobile 073-511-9154, maritabergman@bredband.net).

BY BIKE

To tour Stockholm on two wheels, you can either use one of the city bikes or rent your own.

Using City Bikes: Stockholm's City Bikes program is a good option for seeing this bike-friendly town. While you'll find similar bike-sharing programs all over Europe, Stockholm's is the

most usable and helpful for travelers. It's easy, the bikes are great, and the city lends itself to joy-riding.

Purchase a 165-kr, three-day City Bike card at the TI, at the SL Center (Stockholm Transport) office at Sergels Torg, or at many hotels and hostels. The card allows you to grab a bike from one of the more than 90 City Bike racks around the city. You must return it within three hours (to any rack), but if you want to keep riding, just check out another bike. You can do this over and over for three days (available April-Oct only, www.citybikes.se).

The downside: Unless you have a lock, you can't park your bike as you sightsee. You'll need to return it to a station and get another when you're ready to go—which sounds easy enough, but in practice many stations are full (without an empty port in which to leave a bike) or have no bikes available. To overcome this problem, download the fun, easy, and free app from the website, which can help you find the nearest racks and bikes.

Renting a Bike: You can also rent bikes (and boats) at **Sjö-caféet,** next to Djurgårdsbron bridge near the Vasa Museum. It's ideally situated as a springboard for a pleasant bike ride around the park-like Djurgården island—use their free and excellent bike map/guide.

Stockholm Walks

This section includes two different self-guided walks to introduce you to Stockholm, both old (Gamla Stan) and new (the modern city).

▲▲OLD TOWN (GAMLA STAN) WALK

Stockholm's historic island core is charming, photogenic, and full of antiques shops, street lanterns, painted ceilings, and surprises. Until the 1600s, all of Stockholm fit in Gamla Stan. Stockholm traded with other northern ports such as Amsterdam, Lübeck, and Tallinn. German culture influenced art, building styles, and even the language, turning Old Norse into modern Swedish. With its narrow alleys and stairways, Gamla Stan mixes poorly with cars and modern economies. Today, it's been given over to the Royal Palace and to the tourists, who throng Gamla Stan's main drag, Västerlånggatan, seemingly unaware that most of Stockholm's best attractions are elsewhere. While you could just

STOCKHOLM

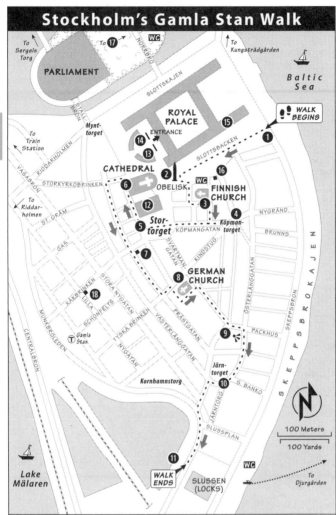

Stockholm's Gamla Stan Walk

Self-Guided Walk
1. King Gustav III Statue
2. Obelisk
3. Iron Boy Statue
4. St. George Statue
5. Stortorget
6. Cathedral
7. Rune Stone
8. German Church
9. Viewpoint
10. Järntorget
11. Bridge & Lock

Additional Sights
12. Nobel Museum
13. Palace Info Booth
14. Changing of the Guard
15. Royal Armory
16. Royal Coin Cabinet & Swedish Economic Museum
17. To Museum of Medieval Stockholm
18. The English Bookshop

happily wander, this quick walk gives meaning to Stockholm's Old Town.

• *Our walk begins along the harborfront. Start at the base of Slotts-backen (the Palace Hill esplanade) leading up to the...*

Royal Palace: Along the water, check out the ❶ **statue of King Gustav III** gazing at the palace, which was built on the site of Stockholm's first castle (described later, under "Sights in Stockholm"). Gustav turned Stockholm from a dowdy Scandinavian port into a sophisticated European capital, modeled on French culture. Gustav loved the arts, and he founded the Royal Dramatic Theater and the Royal Opera in Stockholm. Ironically, he was assassinated at a masquerade ball at the Royal Opera House in 1792, inspiring Verdi's opera *Un Ballo in Maschera*.

Walk up the broad, cobbled boulevard to the crest of the hill. Stop, look back, and scan the harbor. The grand building across

the water is the National Museum, which is often mistaken for the palace. Beyond that, in the distance, is the fine row of buildings on Strandvägen street. Until the 1850s, this area was home to peasant shacks, but as Stockholm entered its grand stage, it was cleaned up and replaced by fine apartments, including some of the city's smartest addresses. The blocky gray TV tower—a major attraction back in the 1970s—stands tall in the distance. Turn to the palace facade on your left (finished in 1754, replacing one that burned in 1697). The niches are filled with Swedish bigwigs (literally) from the mid-18th century.

As you crest the hill, you're facing the ❷ **obelisk** that honors Stockholm's merchant class for its support in a 1788 war against Russia. In front of the obelisk are tour buses (their drivers worried about parking cops) and a sand pit used for *boules*. The royal family took a liking to the French game during a Mediterranean vacation, and it's quite popular around town today. Behind the obelisk stands Storkyrkan, Stockholm's cathedral (which we'll visit later in this walk). From this angle you can see its Baroque facade, which was added to

better match the newer palace. Opposite the palace (dark orange building on left) is the Finnish church (Finska Kyrkan), which originated as the royal tennis hall. When the Protestant Refor-

STOCKHOLM

mation hit in 1527, church services could at last be said in the peoples' languages rather than Latin. Suddenly, each merchant community needed its own church. Finns worshiped here, the Germans built their own church (coming up on this walk), and the Swedes got the cathedral.

Stroll up the lane to the right of the Finnish church into the shady churchyard where you'll find the fist-sized ❸ *Iron Boy,* the tiniest

public statue (out of about 600 statues) in Stockholm. Swedish grannies knit caps for him in the winter. Local legend says the statue honors the orphans who had to transfer cargo from sea ships to lake ships before Stockholm's locks were built. Some people rub his head for good luck (which the orphans didn't have). Others, likely needy when it comes to this gift, rub his head for wisdom. The artist says it's simply a self-portrait of himself as a child, sitting on his bed and gazing at the moon.

• *Continue through the yard, turn left onto Trädgårdsgatan, then bear right with the lane until you pop out at...*

Köpmangatan: Take a moment to explore this street from one end to the other. With its cobbles and traditional pastel facades, this is a quintessential Gamla Stan lane—and one of the oldest in town. The mellow yellow houses are predominantly from the 18th century; the red facades are mostly 17th century. Once merchants' homes, today these are popular with antique dealers. Back when there was comfort living within a city's walls, Gamla Stan streets like this were densely populated.

Head left, and you'll emerge on Köpmantorget square, with the breathtaking ❹ **statue of St. George** slaying the dragon. About 10 steps to the right of that is a maiden (representing Stockholm), looking on with thanks and admiration. At the other (top) end of the lane is old Stockholm's main square, our next stop.

❺ **Stortorget, Stockholm's Oldest Square:** Colorful old buildings topped with gables line this square, which was the heart of medieval Stockholm (pop. 6,000 in 1400). This was where the many tangled lanes intersected, becoming the natural center for shopping and the town well. Today Stortorget is home to lots of tourists—including a steady storm of cruise groups following the numbered Ping-Pong paddle

of their guides on four-hour blitz tours of the city (300 ships call here between June and September each year). The square also hosts concerts, occasional demonstrators, and—in winter—Christmas shoppers at an outdoor market.

The grand building on the right is the **Stock Exchange.** It now houses the noble Nobel Museum (described later, under "Sights in Stockholm"). On the immediate left is the social-services agency **Stockholms Stadsmission** (offering the cheapest and best lunch around at the recommended Grillska Huset). If you peek into the adjacent bakery, you'll get a fine look at the richly decorated ceilings characteristic of Gamla Stan in the 17th century—the exotic flowers and animals implied that the people who lived or worked here were worldly. You'll also spy some tempting marzipan cakes (a local favorite) and *kanelbullar* (cinnamon buns). There's a cheap sandwich counter in the back and lots of picnic benches in the square.

The town well is still a popular meeting point. This square long held the town's pillory. Scan the fine old facades. The site of the **Stockholm Bloodbath** of 1520, this square has a notorious history. During a Danish power grab, many of Stockholm's movers and shakers who had challenged Danish rule—Swedish aristocracy, leading merchants, and priests—were rounded up, brought here, and beheaded. Rivers of blood were said to have flowed through the streets. Legend holds that the 80 or so white stones in the fine red facade across the square symbolize the victims. (One victim's son escaped, went into hiding, and resurfaced to lead a Swedish revolt against the Danish rulers. Three years later, the Swedes elected that rebel, Gustav Vasa, as their first king. He went on to usher in a great period in the country's history—the Swedish Renaissance.)

• *At the far end of the square (under the finest gables), turn right and follow Trångsund toward the cathedral.*

❻ Cathedral (Storkyrkan): Just before the church, you'll see my personal phone booth (Rikstelefon) and the gate to the churchyard—guarded by statues of Caution and Hope. Enter the yellow-brick church—Stockholm's oldest, from the 13th century (40 kr; daily 9:00-16:00, open later Mon-Fri in summer—until 17:00 or 18:00). Signs explain events (busy with tours and services in summer).

When buying your ticket, pick up the free, worthwhile English-language flier. Exploring the cathedral's interior, you'll find many styles, ranging from medieval to modern. The front of the nave is paved with centuries-old **tombstones.** At one time, more than a thousand people were buried under the church. The tombstone of the Swedish reformer Olaus Petri is appropriately simple and appropriately located—under the finely carved and gilded pulpit. A witness to the Stockholm Bloodbath, Petri was nearly executed himself. He went on to befriend Gustav Vasa and guide him in Lutheranizing Sweden (and turning this cathedral from Catholic to Protestant). The fine 17th-century altar is made of silver and ebony. Above it, the silver Christ stands like a conquering general evoking the 1650s, an era of Swedish military might.

Opposite the pulpit, find the **bronze plaque** in the pillar. It recalls the 1925 Swedish-led ecumenical meeting of all Christian leaders—except the pope—that encouraged the Church to speak out against the type of evil that resulted in World War I's horrific death toll.

The **royal boxes** (carved wood, between the pulpit and the altar) date from 1684. In June of 2010, this church hosted a royal wedding (Crown Princess Victoria, heir to the throne, married Daniel Westling, her personal trainer). Imagine the pomp and circumstance as the nation's attention was drawn to this spot.

The remarkably detailed **statue** to the left of the altar, *Saint George and the Dragon* (1489)—a copy of which you saw outside a few minutes ago—is carved of oak and elk horn. To some, this symbolizes the Swedes' overcoming the evil Danes (commemorating a military victory in 1471). In a broader sense, it's an inspiration to take up the struggle against even non-Danish evil. Regardless, it must be the gnarliest dragon's head in all of Europe.

Return to the back of the church to find the exit. Before leaving, just to the left of the door, notice the **painting** that depicts Stockholm in the early 1500s, showing a walled city filling only today's Gamla Stan. It's a 1630 copy of the 1535 original. The church with its black spire dominated the town back then. The strange sun and sky predicted big changes in Sweden—and as a matter of fact, that's what happened. Gustav Vasa brought on huge reforms in religion and beyond. (The doors just to the left and right of the painting lead to a free WC.)

Heading outside, you'll emerge into the kid-friendly churchyard, which was once the cemetery.

• *With your back to the church's front door, turn right and continue down*

Trångsund. At the next corner, turn left and ...
brinken and take the first left on...

Prästgatan: Enjoy a quiet wander (
century "Priests' Lane." Västerlånggatan
allels this lane one block over. (While ...

walk back up it ...
walk.) As you stroll Prästgatan, look for
bits of its past: hoists poking out horizon-
tally from gables (merchants used these to
lift goods into their attics), tie bolts (iron
bars necessary to bind the timber beams
of tall buildings together), small coal or
wood hatches (for fuel delivery back in the
good old days), and flaming gold phoe-
nixes under red-crown medallions (telling
firefighters which houses paid insurance
and could be saved in case of fire—for example, #46). Like other Scandinavian cities, Stockholm was plagued by fire until it
was finally decreed that only stone, stucco, and brick construction
(like you see here) would be allowed in the town center.

After a few blocks (at Kåkbrinken), a cannon barrel on the
corner (look down) guards a Viking-age ❼ **rune stone.** In case you
can't read the old Nordic script, it says: "Torsten and Frogun erected this stone in memory of their son."

• *Continue one block farther down Prästgatan to Tyska Brinken and*
turn left. You will see the powerful brick steeple of the German Church.

❽ **German Church** (Tyska Kyrkan): The church's carillon has
played four times a day since 1666. Think of the days when German merchants worked here. Today, Germans come to Sweden not
to run the economy, but to enjoy its pristine nature (which is pro-
gressively harder to find in their own crowded homeland). Sweden
formally became a Lutheran country even before the northern part
of Germany—making this the very first German Lutheran church
(free, Mon-Sat 11:00-15:00, Sun 12:30-17:00).

• *Wander through the churchyard (past a cute church café) and out the*
back. Exit right onto Svartmangatan and follow it to the right, ending
at an iron railing overlooking Österlånggatan.

❾ **Viewpoint:** From this perch, survey the street below to the
left and right. Notice how it curves. This marks the old shoreline.
In medieval times, piers stretched out like fingers into the harbor.
Gradually, as land was reclaimed and developed, these piers were
extended, becoming lanes leading to piers farther away. Behind you
is a cute shop where elves can actually be seen making elves.

• *Walk right along Österlånggatan to...*

❿ **Järntorget:** A customs square in medieval times, this was

ˌof Sweden's first bank back in 1680 (the yellow build-
ˌ the bars on the windows). The Co-op Nära supermarket
ˌs square offers picnic fixings. From here, Västerlånggatan—
ˌ eating, shopping, and commercial pedestrian mall of Gamla
ˌtan—leads back across the island. You'll be there in a minute, but
first finish this walk.

• *Continue out of the square (opposite where you entered) down Järn-torgsgatan, walk (carefully) out into the traffic hell, passing an eques-trian statue of Jean-Baptiste Bernadotte—the French son of a lawyer invited to establish the current Swedish royal dynasty in the early 1800s. Continue ahead 50 yards until you reach a viewpoint overlooking a lock.*

❶ **Bridge Overlooking Slussen:** This area is called Slus-sen, named for the locks between the salt water of the Baltic Sea (to your left) and the fresh water of the huge Lake Mälaren (to your right). In fact, Stockholm exists because this is where Lake Mälaren meets the sea. Traders would sail their goods from far inland to this point, where they'd meet merchants who would ship the goods south to Europe. In the 13th century, the new King-dom of Sweden needed revenue, and began levying duty taxes on all the iron, copper, and furs shipped through here. From the bridge, you may notice a current in the water, indicating that the weir has been lowered and water is spilling from Lake Mälaren (about two feet above sea level) into the sea. Today, the locks are nicknamed "the divorce lock" because this is where captains and first mates learn to communicate under pressure and in the public eye.

Survey the view. Opposite Gamla Stan is the island of **Söder-malm**—bohemian, youthful, artsy, and casual—with its popular Katarina viewing platform. Moored on the saltwater side are the cruise ships, which bring thousands of visitors into town each day during the season. Many of these boats are bound for Finland. The towering white syringe is the Gröna Lund amusement park's free-fall ride. The revolving *Djurgården Färjan* sign, along the embank-ment to your left, marks the ferry that zips from here directly to Gröna Lund and Djurgården.

You could catch bus #2, which heads back downtown (the stop is just beyond Bernadotte, next to the waterfront). But better yet, linger longer in Gamla Stan—day or night, it's a lively place to enjoy. Västerlånggatan, Gamla Stan's main commercial drag, is a touristy festival of distractions that keeps most visitors from seeing the historic charms of the Old Town—which you just did. Now you're free to window-shop and eat. Or, if it's late, find some live music.

• *For more sightseeing, consider the other sights in Gamla Stan or at the Royal Palace (all described later, under "Sights in Stockholm"). If you continue back up Västerlånggatan (always going straight), you'll reach*

Fika: **Sweden's Coffee Break**

Swedes drink more coffee per capita than just about any other country in the world. The Swedish coffee break—or *fika*—is a ritual. *Fika* is to Sweden what tea-time is to Britain. The typical *fika* is a morning or afternoon break in the workday, but can happen any time, any day. It's the perfect opportunity (and excuse) for tourists to take a break as well.

Fika fare is coffee with a snack—something sweet or savory. Your best bet is a *kanelbulle*, a Swedish cinnamon bun, although some prefer *pariserbulle*, a bun filled with vanilla cream. These can be found nearly everywhere coffee is sold, including just about any café or *konditori* (bakery) in Stockholm. A coffee and a cinnamon bun in a café will cost you about 40 kr. (Most cafés will give you a coffee refill for free.) But at Pressbyrån, the Swedish convenience stores found all over town, you can satisfy your *fika* fix for 25 kr by getting a coffee and bun to go. Grab a park bench or waterside perch, relax, and enjoy.

STOCKHOLM

the Parliament building and cross the water back over onto Norrmalm (where the street becomes Drottninggatan). This pedestrian street leads back into Stockholm's modern, vibrant new town.

From here it's also a 10-minute walk to Kungsträdgården, the starting point of my Modern City self-guided walk (described next). You can either walk along the embankment and take the diagonal bridge directly across to the square, or you can walk back through the middle of Gamla Stan, taking the stately walkway past the Parliament, then turning right when you cross the bridge. On the way there, you'll pass the Royal Opera House and (tucked behind it) Gustav Adolfs Torg, with its imposing statue of Gustavus Adolphus. He was the king who established the Swedish empire. Considered by many to be the father of modern warfare for his innovative tactics, he was a Protestant hero of the Thirty Years' War.

STOCKHOLM'S MODERN CITY WALK

On this walk, we'll use the park called Kungsträdgården as a springboard to explore the modern center of Stockholm—a commercial zone designed to put the focus not on old kings and mementos of superpower days, but on shopping.

• *Find the statue of King Karl XII, facing the waterfront at the harbor end of the park.*

Kungsträdgården: Centuries ago, this "King's Garden" was the private kitchen garden of the king, where he grew his cabbage salad. Today, this downtown people-watching center, worth ▲, is

considered Stockholm's living room, symbolizing the Swedes' freedom-loving spirit. While the name implies that the garden is a private royal domain, the giant clump of elm trees just behind the statue reminds locals that it's the people who rule now. In the 1970s, demonstrators chained themselves to these trees to stop the building of an underground train station here. They prevailed, and today, locals enjoy the peaceful, breezy ambience of a teahouse instead. Watch the AstroTurf zone with "latte dads" and their kids, and enjoy a summer concert at the bandstand. There's always something going on. High above is a handy reference point—the revolving NK clock.

Kungsträdgården—surrounded by the harborfront and tour boats, the Royal Opera House, and shopping opportunities (including a welcoming Volvo showroom near the top-left side of the square, showing off the latest in Swedish car design)—is *the* place to feel Stockholm's pulse (but always ask first: *"Kan jag kanna på din puls?"*).

Kungsträdgården also throws huge parties. The Taste of Stockholm festival runs for a week in early June, when restaurateurs show off and bands entertain all day. Beer flows liberally—a rare public spectacle in Sweden.

• *Stroll through Kungsträdgården, past the fountain and the Volvo store, and up to Hamngatan street. From here, we'll turn left and walk the length of the NK department store (across the street) as we wade through...*

Stockholm's Urban Shopping Zone (Hamngatan): In just a couple of blocks, we'll pass some major landmarks of Swedish consumerism. First, at the top of Kungsträdgården on the left, look for the gigantic **Illums Bolighus** design shop. (You can enter from the square and stroll all the way through it, popping out at Hamngatan on the far end.) This is a Danish institution, making its play for Swedish customers with this prime location. Across the street (on your right as you walk down Hamngatan), notice the giant gold *NK* marking the **Nordiska Kompaniet** department store (locals joke that the NK stands for "no kronor left"). It's located in an elegant early 20th-century building that dominates the top end of Kungsträdgården. If it feels like an old-time American department store, that's because its architect was inspired by grand stores he'd seen in the US (circa 1910).

Another block down, on the left, is the sleeker, more modern

Gallerian mall. Among this two-story world of shops, upstairs you'll find a Clas Ohlson hardware and electronics shop (a men's favorite, as most Stockholmers have a cabin that's always in need of a little DIY repair). And there are plenty of affordable little lunch bars and classy cafés for your *fika* (Swedish coffee-and-bun break). You may notice that American influence (frozen yogurt and other trendy food chains) is challenging the entire notion of the traditional *fika*.

• *High-end shoppers should consider heading into the streets behind NK, with exclusive designer boutiques and the chichi Mood Stockholm mall. Otherwise, just beyond the huge Gallerian mall, you'll emerge into Sergels Torg. (Note that the handy tram #7 goes from here directly to Skansen and the other important sights on Djurgården; departures every few minutes, tickets sold on board.)*

Sergels Torg and Kulturhuset: Sergels Torg square, worth ▲, dominates the heart of modern Stockholm with its stark 1960s-era functionalist architecture. The glassy tower in the middle of the fountain plaza is ugly in daylight but glows at night, symbolic of Sweden's haunting northern lights.

Kulturhuset, the hulking, low-slung, glassy building overlooking the square (on your left) is Stockholm's "culture center." Inside, just past the welcoming info desk, you'll find a big model of the city that locals use to check in on large infrastructure projects. Push a few buttons and see what's happening. In this lively cultural zone, there's a space for kids, a library (with magazines and computer terminals), chessboards, fun shops, fine art cinema, art exhibits, and a venue for new bands (tel. 08/5083-1508, www.kulturhuset.stockholm.se).

I like to take the elevator to the top and explore each level by riding the escalator back down to the ground floor. On the rooftop, choose from one of two recommended eateries with terrific city views: Cafeteria Panorama has cheap meals and a salad bar while the Mat and Bar café is trendier and pricier.

Back outside, stand in front of the Kulturhuset (across from the fountain) and survey the expansive square nicknamed "Plattan" (the platter). Everything around you dates from the 1960s and 1970s, when this formerly run-down area was reinvented as an urban "space of the future." In the 1970s, with no nearby residences, the desolate Plattan became the domain of junkies. Now the city is actively revitalizing it, and the Plattan is becoming a people-friendly heart of the commercial town.

DesignTorget (enter from the lower level of Kulturhuset) is a place for independent Swedish designers to showcase and sell their clever products. (Local designers submit their creations, and the DesignTorget staff votes on and carries their favorites—perhaps you need a banana case?) Nearby are the major boutiques and department stores, including, across the way, H&M and Åhléns.

Sergelgatan, a thriving pedestrian and commercial street, leads past the five uniform white towers you see beyond the fountain. These office towers, so modern in the 1960s, have gone from seeming hopelessly out-of-date to being considered "retro," and are now quite popular with young professionals.

• *Walk up Sergelgatan past the towers, enjoying the public art and people-watching, to the market at Hötorget.*

Hötorget: "Hötorget" means "Hay Market," but today its stalls feed people rather than horses. The adjacent indoor market, Hötorgshallen, is fun and fragrant. It dates from 1914 when, for hygienic reasons, the city forbade selling fish and meat outdoors. Carl Milles' statue of *Orpheus Emerging from the Underworld* (with seven sad Muses) stands in front of the city concert hall (which hosts the annual Nobel Prize award ceremony). The concert

house, from 1926, is Swedish Art Deco (a.k.a. "Swedish Grace"). The lobby (open through much of the summer, 70-kr tours) still evokes Stockholm's Roaring Twenties. If the door's open, you're welcome to look in for free.

Popping into the Hötorget T-bana station provides a fun glimpse at local urban design. Stockholm's subway system was inaugurated in the 1950s, and many stations are modern art installations in themselves.

• *Our walk ends here. For more shopping and an enjoyable pedestrian boulevard leading back into the Old Town, cut down a block to Drottninggatan and turn left. This busy drag leads straight out of the commercial district, passes the Parliament, then becomes the main street of Gamla Stan.*

Sights in Stockholm

GAMLA STAN (OLD TOWN)

The best of Gamla Stan is covered in my self-guided "Old Town Walk," earlier. But here are a few ways to extend your time in the Old Town.

On Stortorget
▲Nobel Museum (Nobelmuseet)

Opened in 2001 for the 100-year anniversary of the Nobel Prize, this wonderful little museum tells the story of the world's most prestigious prize. Pricey but high-tech and eloquent, it fills the grand old stock exchange building that dominates Gamla Stan's main square, Stortorget.

Cost and Hours: 100 kr, free Tue after 17:00; open June-Aug daily 10:00-20:00; Sept-May Tue 11:00-20:00, Wed-Sun 11:00-17:00, closed Mon; audioguide-20 kr, free 30-minute orientation tours in English: 6/day in summer, fewer off-season; on Stortorget in the center of Gamla Stan a block from the Royal Palace, tel. 08/5348-1800, www.nobelmuseum.se.

Background: Stockholm-born Alfred Nobel was a great inventor, with more than 300 patents. His most famous invention: dynamite. Living in the late 1800s, Nobel was a man of his age. It was a time of great optimism, wild ideas, and grand projects. His dynamite enabled entire nations to blast their way into the modern age with canals, railroads, and tunnels. It made warfare much more destructive. And it also made Alfred Nobel a very wealthy man. Wanting to leave a legacy that celebrated and supported people with great ideas, Alfred used his fortune to fund the Nobel Prize. Every year since 1901, laureates have been honored in the fields of physics, chemistry, medicine, literature, and peacemaking.

Visiting the Museum: Inside, portraits of all 700-plus prize-winners hang from the ceiling—shuffling around the room like shirts at the dry cleaner's (miss your favorite, and he or she will come around again in six hours). Behind the ticket desk are video screens honoring the six Nobel Prize categories, each running a clip about the most recent laureate in that category.

Flanking the main hall beyond that—where touchscreens organized by decade invite you to learn more about the laureates of your choice—two video rooms run a continuous montage of quick programs (three-minute bios of various winners in one program, five-minute films celebrating various intellectual environments—from Cambridge to Parisian cafés—in the other).

To the right of the ticket desk, find "The Gallery," with an endearingly eccentric collection of items that various laureates have cited as important to their creative process, from scientific equip-

STOCKHOLM

Stockholm at a Glance

▲▲▲**Skansen** Europe's first and best open-air folk museum, with more than 150 old homes, churches, shops, and schools. **Hours:** Park—daily May-late-June 10:00-19:00, late-June-Aug 10:00-22:00, Sept 10:00-18:00, Oct and March-April 10:00-16:00, Nov-Feb 10:00-15:00; historical buildings—generally 11:00-17:00, late June-Aug some until 19:00, most closed in winter. See page 46.

▲▲▲**Vasa Museum** Ill-fated 17th-century warship dredged from the sea floor, now the showpiece of an interesting museum. **Hours:** Daily June-Aug 8:30-18:00; Sept-May 10:00-17:00 except Wed until 20:00. See page 48.

▲▲**Military Parade and Changing of the Guard** Punchy pomp starting near Nybroplan and finishing at Royal Palace outer courtyard. **Hours:** Mid-May-mid-Sept daily, mid-Sept-April Wed and Sat-Sun only, start time varies with season but always at midday. See page 34.

▲▲**Royal Armory** A fine collection of ceremonial medieval royal armor, historic and modern royal garments, and carriages, in the Royal Palace. **Hours:** May-June daily 11:00-17:00; July-Aug daily 10:00-18:00; Sept-April Tue-Sun 11:00-17:00, Thu until 20:00, closed Mon. See page 35.

▲▲**City Hall** Gilt mosaic architectural jewel of Stockholm and site of Nobel Prize banquet, with tower offering the city's best views. **Hours:** Required tours daily generally June-Aug every 30 minutes 9:30-16:00, off-season hourly 10:00-15:00. See page 40.

▲▲**Nordic Museum** Danish Renaissance palace design and five fascinating centuries of traditional Swedish lifestyles. **Hours:** Daily 10:00-17:00, Wed until 20:00 Sept-May. See page 51.

ment to inspirational knickknacks. The randomness of the items offers a fascinating and humanizing insight into the great minds of our time. Beyond that are a room dedicated to Alfred Nobel and a small children's area.

The Viennese-style Bistro Nobel is the place to get creative with your coffee...and sample the famous Nobel ice cream. All Nobel laureates who visit the museum are asked to sign the bottom of a chair in the café. Turn yours over and see who warmed your chair. And don't miss the lockable hangers, to protect your fancy, furry winter coat. The Swedish Academy, which awards the Nobel Prize for literature each year, is upstairs.

▲**Nobel Museum** Star-studded tribute to some of the world's most accomplished scientists, artists, economists, and politicians. **Hours:** June-Aug daily 10:00-20:00; Sept-May Tue 11:00-20:00, Wed-Sun 11:00-17:00; closed Mon. See page 31.

▲**Royal Palace Museums** Complex of Swedish royal museums, the two best of which are the Royal Apartments and Royal Treasury. **Hours:** Mid-May-mid-Sept daily 10:00-17:00; mid-Sept-mid-May Tue-Sun 12:00-16:00, closed Mon. See page 36.

▲**Royal Coin Cabinet** Europe's best look at the history of money, with a sweep through the evolution of the Swedish economy to boot. **Hours:** Daily June-Aug 11:00-17:00, Sept-May 10:00-16:00. See page 38.

▲**Kungsträdgården** Stockholm's lively central square, with life-size chess games, concerts, and perpetual action. **Hours:** Always open. See page 27.

▲**Sergels Torg** Modern square with underground mall. **Hours:** Always open. See page 29.

▲**ABBA: The Museum** A super-commercial and wildly-popular-with-ABBA-fans experience. **Hours:** Daily 10:00-20:00, shorter hours off-season. See page 52.

▲**Thielska Galleriet** Enchanting waterside mansion with works of Scandinavian artists Larsson, Zorn, and Munch. **Hours:** Tue-Sun 12:00-17:00, closed Mon. See page 54.

▲**Millesgården** Dramatic cliffside museum and grounds featuring works of Sweden's greatest sculptor, Carl Milles. **Hours:** Daily 11:00-17:00 except closed Mon in Oct-April. See page 56.

STOCKHOLM

Royal Palace Complex (Kungliga Slottet)

Although the royal family beds down at Drottningholm, this complex in Gamla Stan is still the official royal residence. The palace, designed in Italian Baroque style, was completed in 1754 after a fire wiped out the previous palace—a much more characteristic medieval/Renaissance complex. This blocky Baroque replacement, which houses various museums, is big and (frankly) pretty dull. Note two of the sights—the Royal Armory and the Royal Coin Cabinet—are operated by different organizations, so they have separate entrances and tickets.

Planning Your Time: Visiting the several sights in and near

STOCKHOLM

the palace could fill a day, but Stockholm has far better attractions elsewhere. Prioritize. The Changing of the Guard and the awesome Royal Armory are the highlights.

The Royal Palace ticket includes four museums. Of these, the Royal Treasury is worth a look; the Royal Apartments are not much as far as palace rooms go; the Museum of Three Crowns gets you down into the medieval cellars to learn about the more interesting earlier castle; and Gustav III's Museum of Antiquities is skippable. The chapel is nice enough (and the only interior that's free to enter). The Royal Coin Cabinet—which requires a separate ticket—fascinates coin collectors.

Visitors in a rush should see the Changing of the Guard, pay to enter the Royal Armory, and skip the rest. The information booth in the semicircular courtyard (at the top, where the guard changes) gives out a list of the day's guided tours and an explanatory brochure/map that marks the entrances to the different sights. The main entrance to the Royal Palace (including the apartments, chapel, and treasury) faces the long, angled square and obelisk.

Tours: In peak season, the main Royal Palace offers a full slate of English tours covering the different sights (included in the admission)—allowing you to systematically cover nearly the entire complex. If you're paying the hefty price for a ticket, you might as well try to join at least one of the tours—otherwise, you'll struggle to appreciate the place. Some tours are infrequent, so be sure to confirm times when you purchase your admission (for more on tours, see the individual listings below).

Expect Changes: Since the palace is used for state functions, it is sometimes closed to tourists. And, as the exterior is undergoing a 20-year renovation, don't be surprised if parts are covered in scaffolding.

▲▲Military Parade and Changing of the Guard

Starting two blocks from Nybroplan (in front of the Army Museum at Riddargatan 13), Stockholm's daily military parade marches

over Norrbro bridge, in front of the Parliament building, and up to the Royal Palace's outer courtyard, where the band plays and the guard changes. Smaller contingents of guards spiral in from other parts of the palace complex, eventually convening in the same place.

The performance is fresh and spirited, because the soldiers are visiting Stockholm just like you—and it's a chance for young soldiers from all over Sweden in every branch of the service to show their stuff in the big city. Pick

your place at the palace courtyard, where the band arrives at about 12:15 (13:15 on Sun). The best spot to stand is along the wall in the inner courtyard, near the palace information and ticket office. There are columns with wide pedestals for easy perching, as well as benches that people stand on to view the ceremony (arrive early). Generally, after the barking and goose-stepping formalities, the band shows off for an impressive 30-minute marching concert. Though the royal family now lives out of town at Drottningholm, the palace guards are for real. If the guard by the cannon in the semicircular courtyard looks a little lax, try wandering discreetly behind him.

Cost and Hours: Free; mid-May–mid-Sept Mon-Sat parade begins at 11:45 (reaches palace at 12:15), Sun at 12:45 (palace at 13:15); April–mid-May and mid-Sept–Oct Wed and Sat at 11:45 (palace at 12:15), Sun at 12:45 (palace at 13:15); Nov–March starts at palace Wed and Sat at 12:15, Sun at 13:15. Royal appointments can disrupt the schedule; confirm times at TI. In summer, you might also catch the mounted guards (but they do not appear on a regular schedule).

▲▲Royal Armory (Livrustkammaren)

The oldest museum in Sweden is both more and less than an armory. Rather than dusty piles of swords and muskets, it focuses on royal clothing: impressive ceremonial armor (never used in battle) and other fashion through the ages (including a room of kidswear), plus a fine collection of coaches. It's an engaging slice of royal life. Everything is displayed under sturdy brick vaults, beautifully lit, and well-described in English and by the museum's evocative audioguide.

Cost and Hours: 90 kr, half-price if you've already bought your Royal Palace ticket—so if you're touring both sights, buy your palace ticket before you come here; May-June daily 11:00-17:00; July-Aug daily 10:00-18:00; Sept-April Tue-Sun 11:00-17:00, Thu until 20:00, closed Mon; 20-kr audioguide is excellent—romantic couples can share it if they crank up the volume, information sheets in English available in most rooms; entrance at bottom of Slottsbacken at base of palace, tel. 08/402-3010, www.livrustkammaren.se.

Visiting the Museum: Buy your ticket and begin with the ground-floor collection. The first room (A) is almost a shrine for Swedish visitors. It contains the clothes **Gustavus Adolphus** wore—and even the horse he was riding, when he was killed in the

Thirty Years' War. Continue through Room B into Rooms C and D, where the exquisite workmanship on the **ceremonial armor** is a fine example of weaponry as an art form. Also in Room D are **royal suits and gowns** through the ages. The 1766 wedding dress of Queen Sofia is designed to cleverly show off its fabulously rich fabric (the dress seems even wider when compared to her 20-inch corseted waist). There are some modern dresses here as well. The **royal children** get a section for themselves (Room E), featuring a cradle that has rocked heirs to the throne since the 1650s; eventually it will leave the armory to rock the next royal offspring as well. It's fun to imagine little princes romping around their 600-room home with these toys. A century ago, one prince treasured his box-car and loved playing cowboys and Indians. At the end of the main hall is a children's area.

The easy-to-miss **mezzanine level** (overlooking these main rooms) is typically filled with good temporary exhibits.

Backtrack to the entrance and find the stairs down to the basement, filled with lavish **royal coaches.** The highlight (last coach on the right, with purple and blue accents) is a plush coronation coach made in France in about 1700 and shipped to Stockholm, ready to be assembled Ikea-style. It last rolled a king to his big day—with its eight fine horses and what was then the latest in suspension gear—in 1869. At the end of the hall, the display of luggage over the centuries makes it obvious that Swedish royalty didn't know how to pack light.

▲Royal Palace

The Royal Palace consists of a chapel and four museums. Compared to many grand European palaces, it's underwhelming and flooded with cruise-excursion groups who don't realize that Stockholm's best sightseeing is elsewhere. It's worth a quick walk-through if you have a Stockholm Card (and, as a bonus, cardholders can go straight into each museum, bypassing the ticket office).

Cost and Hours: 150-kr combo-ticket covers all four museums and the chapel, includes guided tour; mid-May-mid-Sept daily 10:00-17:00; mid-Sept-mid-May Tue-Sun 12:00-16:00, closed Mon; tel. 08/402-6130, www.royalcourt.se.

Orientation: I've listed the museums in order of sightseeing worthiness. But if you want to see them all with minimal backtracking, follow this plan: Begin at the main entrance. Head up to the chapel for a peek, then descend to the treasury. Tour the Royal Apartments, exiting at the far side of the building—where you can head straight into the Museum of Three Crowns. Exiting there, you'll find the final sight (Museum of Antiquities) to your right.

Royal Apartments: The stately palace exterior encloses 608 rooms (one more than Britain's Buckingham Palace) of glittering

18th-century Baroque and Rococo decor. Clearly the palace of Scandinavia's superpower, it's steeped in royal history. You'll enter into the grand main hall (cheapskates can get a free look at this first room before reaching the ticket checkpoint), then walk the long halls through four sections. On the main level are the Hall of State (with an exhibit of fancy state awards) and the lavish Bernadotte Apartments (some fine Rococo interiors and portraits of the Bernadotte dynasty); upstairs you'll find the State Apartments (with rooms dating to the 1690s—darker halls, faded tapestries, and a wannabe hall of mirrors) and the Guest Apartments (with less lavish quarters, where visiting heads of state still crash). Guided 45-minute **tours** in English run twice daily.

Royal Treasury (Skattkammaren): Refreshingly compact compared to the sprawling apartments, the treasury gives you a good, up-close look at Sweden's crown jewels. Climbing down into the super-secure vault, you'll see 12 cases filled with fancy crowns, scepters, jeweled robes, the silver baptismal font of Karl XI, and plenty of glittering gold. It's particularly worthwhile with an English guided **tour** (daily at 13:00) or the included **audioguide** (which covers basically the same information). The first room holds the crowns of princes and princesses, while the second shows off the more serious regalia of kings and queens. For more than a century, these crowns have gone unworn: The last Swedish coronation was Oskar II's in 1873; in 1907 his son and successor—out of deference for the constitution (and living in a Europe that was deep in the throes of modernism)—declined to wear the crown, so he was "enthroned" rather than "coronated." The crowns still belong to the monarchs and are present in the room on special occasions—but they are symbols rather than accessories.

Museum of Three Crowns (Museum Tre Kronor): This museum shows off bits of the palace from before a devastating 1697 fire. The models, illustrations, and artifacts are displayed in vaulted medieval cellars that are far more evocative than the run-of-the-mill interior of today's palace. But while the stroll through the cellars is atmospheric, it's basically just more old stuff, interesting only to real history buffs (guided tours in English offered on summer afternoons).

Chapel: If you don't want to spring for a ticket, but would like a little taste of palace opulence, climb the stairs inside the main entrance for a peek into the chapel—the only free sight at the palace. It's standard-issue royal Baroque: colorful ceiling painting, bubbly altars, and a giant organ.

Gustav III's Museum of Antiquities (Gustav III's Antikmuseum): In the 1700s, Gustav III traveled through Italy and brought home an impressive gallery of classical Roman statues. These are displayed exactly as they were in the 1790s. This was a huge deal for those who had never been out of Sweden (English tour at 16:00).

▲Royal Coin Cabinet (Kungliga Myntkabinettet)

More than your typical royal coin collection, this is the best money museum I've seen in Europe. A fine exhibit tells the story of money from crude wampum to credit cards, and traces the development of the modern Swedish economy. The mellow but informative included audioguide helps make sense of the collection (which has only some English descriptions).

Cost and Hours: 70 kr, free on Mon, open daily June-Aug 11:00-17:00, Sept-May 10:00-16:00, Slottsbacken 6, tel. 08/5195-5304, www.myntkabinettet.se.

Visiting the Museum: You'll begin on the ground floor, with a chronological sweep through the history of money, starting with the first-ever coin (look for the tiny, easy-to-miss golden pellet labeled *det första myntet*, dating from 625 B.C.). The gang's all here: the ancient Greek drachma, the Roman dinarius, Charlemagne's denier, Florence's florin, ducats, pesos...and the German taler, where our dollar got its name. Banknotes finally arrived on the scene in 1661.

The upper floors are less engaging: The first floor up is heavy on Swedish economic history, including an interesting exhibit on "plate money"—from a time when, rather than bags of small coins, merchants carried around 40-pound slabs of copper (try to lift one). The second floor has the small royal coin collection and a large exhibit on ceremonial medals—including an actual Nobel Prize. The "Tally Up!" exhibit examines the role of money in our contemporary world, where the gulf between rich and poor seems greater than ever.

More Gamla Stan Sights

These first two sights sit on the Gamla Stan islet of Helgeandsholmen (just north of the Royal Palace), which is dominated by the Swedish Parliament. Also at the edge of Gamla Stan is the stately island of Riddarholmen.

Parliament (Riksdag)

For a firsthand look at Sweden's government, tour the Parliament buildings. Guides enjoy a chance to teach a little Swedish poli-sci along the standard tour of the building and its art. It's also possible to watch the Parliament in session.

Cost and Hours: Free one-hour tours go in English late June-late Aug, usually 4/day Mon-Fri (when Parliament is not in session). The rest of the year tours run 1/day Sat-Sun only; you're also welcome to join Swedish citizens in the viewing gallery (free); enter at Riksgatan 3a, call 08/786-4862 between 9:00 and 11:00 to confirm tour times, www.riksdagen.se.

Museum of Medieval Stockholm (Medeltidsmuseet)

This modern, well-presented museum offers a look at medieval Stockholm. When the government was digging a parking garage near the Parliament building in the 1970s, workers uncovered a major archaeological find: parts of the town wall that King Gustav Vasa built in the 1530s, as well as a churchyard. This underground museum preserves these discoveries and explains how Stockholm grew from a medieval village to a major city, with a focus on its interactions with fellow Hanseatic League trading cities. Lots of artifacts, models, life-size dioramas, and sound and lighting effects—all displayed in a vast subterranean space—help bring the story to life.

The museum does a particularly good job of profiling individuals who lived in medieval Stockholm; their personal stories vividly set the context of the history. You'll also see the preserved remains of a small cannon-ship from the 1520s and a reconstructed main market square from 13th-century Stockholm.

Cost and Hours: 100 kr ticket normally includes Stockholm City Museum in Södermalm, but that's closed for restoration through 2017, so ticket price may change; Tue-Sun 12:00-17:00, Wed until 19:00, closed Mon; English audioguide-20 kr, enter museum from park in front of Parliament—down below as you cross the bridge, tel. 08/5083-1790, www.medeltidsmuseet.stockholm.se.

Nearby: The museum sits in **Strömparterren** park. With its café and Carl Milles statue of the *Sun Singer* greeting the day, it's a pleasant place for a sightseeing break (pay WC in park, free WC in museum).

Literally the "Knights Isle," Riddarholmen is the quiet and stately far side of Gamla Stan, with a historic church, private palaces, and a famous view. The knights referred to in its name were the nobles who built their palaces on this little island to be near the Royal Palace, just across the way. The island, cut off from the rest of Gamla Stan by a noisy highway, is pretty lifeless, with impersonal government agencies filling its old mansions. Still, a visit is worthwhile for a peek at its church and to enjoy the famous view of City Hall and Lake Mälaren from its far end.

A statue of Birger Jarl (considered the man who founded Stockholm in 1252) marks the main square. Surrounding it are 17th-century private palaces of old noble families (now government buildings). And towering high above is the spire of the Riddarholmen Church. Established in the 13th century as a Franciscan church, this has been the burial place of nearly every Swedish royal since the early 1600s. If you're looking for a Swedish Westminster Abbey, this is it (50 kr, daily 10:00-17:00, shorter hours off-season). An inviting, shady café at the far end of the island is where people (and TV news crews) gather for Riddarholmen's iconic Stockholm view.

DOWNTOWN STOCKHOLM
I've organized these sights and activities in the urban core of Stockholm by island and/or neighborhood.

On Kungsholmen, West of Norrmalm
▲▲City Hall (Stadshuset)
The Stadshuset is an impressive mix of eight million red bricks, 19 million chips of gilt mosaic, and lots of Stockholm pride. While churches dominate cities in southern Europe, in Scandinavian capitals, city halls seem to be the most impressive buildings, celebrating humanism and the ideal of people working together in community. Built in 1923, this is still a functioning city hall. The members of the city council—101 people (mostly women) representing the 850,000 people of Stockholm—are hobby legislators with regular day jobs. That's why they meet in the evening. One of Europe's finest public buildings, the site of the annual Nobel Prize banquet, and a favorite spot for weddings (they do two per hour on Saturday after-

noons, when some parts of the complex may be closed), City Hall is particularly enjoyable and worthwhile for its entertaining and required 50-minute tour.

Cost and Hours: 100 kr; English-only tours offered daily, generally June-Aug every 30 minutes 9:30-16:00, off-season hourly 10:00-15:00; schedule can change due to special events—call to confirm; 300 yards behind the central train station—about a 15-minute walk from either the station or Gamla Stan, bus #3 or #62, tel. 08/5082-9059, www.stockholm.se/cityhall. City Hall's cafeteria, which you enter from the courtyard, serves complete lunches for 95 kr (Mon-Fri 11:00-14:00, closed Sat-Sun).

Visiting City Hall: On the tour, you'll see the building's sumptuous National Romantic style interior (similar to Britain's Arts and Crafts style), celebrating Swedish architecture and craftwork, and created almost entirely with Swedish materials. Highlights include the so-called Blue Hall (the Italian piazza-inspired, loggia-lined courtyard that was originally intended to be open air—hence the name—where the 1,300-plate Nobel banquet takes place); the City Council Chamber (with a gorgeously painted wood-beamed ceiling that resembles a Viking longhouse—or maybe an overturned Viking boat); the Gallery of the Prince (lined with frescoes executed by Prince Eugene of Sweden); and the glittering, gilded, Neo-Byzantine-style, and aptly named Golden Hall, where the Nobel recipients cut a rug after the banquet.

In this over-the-top space, a glimmering mosaic Queen of Lake Mälaren oversees the proceedings with a welcoming but

watchful eye, as East (see Istanbul's Hagia Sophia and the elephant, on the right) and West (notice the skyscrapers with the American flag, on the left) meet here in Stockholm. Above the door across the hall is Sweden's patron saint, Erik, who seems to have lost his head (due to some sloppy mosaic planning). On the tour, you'll find out exactly how many centimeters each Nobel banquet attendee gets at the table, why the building's plans were altered at the last minute to make the tower exactly one meter taller, where the prince got the inspiration for his scenic frescoes, and how the Swedes reacted when they first saw that Golden Hall (hint: they weren't pleased).

▲City Hall Tower

This 348-foot-tall tower rewards those who make the climb with the classic Stockholm view: The old church spires on the atmo-

spheric islands of Gamla Stan pose together, with the rest of the green and watery city spread-eagle around them.

Cost and Hours: 40 kr, daily June-Aug 9:15-17:15, May and Sept 9:15-15:55, closed Oct-April.

Crowd-Beating Tips: Only 30 people at a time are allowed up into the tower, every 40 minutes throughout the day. To ascend, you'll need a timed-entry ticket, which you can only get in person at the tower ticket office on the same day (no phone or Internet orders). It can be a long wait for the next available time, and tickets can sell out by mid-afternoon. If you're touring City Hall, come to the tower ticket window first to see when space is available. Ideally an appointment will coincide with the end of your tour.

Visiting the Tower: A total of 365 steps lead to the top of the tower, but you can ride an elevator partway up—leaving you only 159 easy steps to the top.

First you'll climb up through the brick structure, emerging at an atmospheric hall filled with models of busts and statues that adorn City Hall and a huge, 25-foot-tall statue of St. Erik. The patron saint of Stockholm, Erik was supposed to be hoisted by cranes up through the middle of the tower to stand at its top. But plans changed, big Erik is forever parked halfway up the structure, and the tower's top is open for visitors to gather and enjoy the view.

From Erik, you'll twist gradually up ramps and a few steps at a time through the narrow, labyrinthine brick halls with peek-a-boo views of the city. Finally you'll emerge into the wooden section of the tower, where a spiral staircase brings you up to the roof terrace. Enjoy the view from there, but also take some time to look around at the building's features. Smaller statues of Erik, Klara, Maria Magdalena, and Nikolaus, all patron saints, face their respective parishes. Look up: You're in the company of the tower's nine bells.

On Blasieholmen and Skeppsholmen

The peninsula of Blasieholmen pokes out from downtown Stockholm, and is tethered to the island of Skeppsholmen by a narrow bridge (with great views and adorned with glittering golden crowns). While not connected to the city by T-bana or tram, you can reach this area by bus #65 or the harbor shuttle ferry. Although Skeppsholmen is basically a "dead end" from a transportation perspective, it offers a peaceful break from the bustling city, with glorious views of Gamla Stan on one side and Djurgården on the other.

▲National Museum of Fine Arts (Nationalmuseum)

Stockholm's 200-year-old art museum, though mediocre by European standards, owns a few good pieces. Highlights include several canvases by Rembrandt and Rubens, a fine group of Impressionist works, and a sizeable collection of Russian icons. Seek out the exquisite paintings by the Swedish artists Anders Zorn and Carl Larsson.

Cost and Hours: The museum is

STOCKHOLM

Stockholm's Best Views

For a bird's-eye perspective on this wonderful urban mix of water, parks, concrete, and people, consider these viewpoints.

City Hall Tower: The top of the tower comes with the classic city view (see listing on page 41).

Katarina: This viewing platform—offering fine views over the steeples of Gamla Stan—rises up from Slussen (the busy transit zone between Gamla Stan and Södermalm). You can get to the platform via a pedestrian bridge from Mosebacke Torg, up above in Södermalm. In good summer weather, you'll have to wade through the swanky tables of Eriks restaurant to reach the (free and public) viewpoint.

Himlen: Rising above Södermalm's main drag, the Skrapan skyscraper has a free elevator to the 25th-floor restaurant, called Himlen. While they're hoping you'll buy a meal (200-kr starters, 350-kr main courses) or nurse a 150-kr cocktail in the lounge, it's generally fine to take a discreet peek at the 360-degree views—just march in the door at #78 and ride the elevator up to 25 (daily 14:00-late, Götgatan 78, tel. 08/660-6068, www.restauranghimlen.se).

Kaknäs Tower: This bold, concrete, 500-foot-tall TV tower—looming above the eastern part of the city, and visible from just about everywhere—was once the tallest building in Scandinavia (55 kr, June-Aug Mon-Sat 9:00-22:00, Sun until 19:00, shorter hours off-season, restaurant on 28th floor, east of downtown—bus #69 from Nybroplan or Sergels Torg to Kaknästornet Södra stop, tel. 08/667-2105, www.kaknastornet.se).

closed for an extensive renovation (reopening in 2017); for the latest, see www.nationalmuseum.se.

Museum of Modern Art (Moderna Museet)

This bright, cheery gallery on Skeppsholmen island is as far out as can be. For serious art lovers, it warrants ▲▲. The impressive permanent collection includes modernist all-stars such as Picasso, Braque, Dalí, Matisse, Munch, Kokoschka, and Dix; lots of goofy Dada art (including a copy of Duchamp's urinal); Pollock, Twombly, Bacon, and other postmodern works; and plenty of excellent contemporary stuff as well (don't miss the beloved Rauschenberg *Goat with Tire*).

The curator draws from this substantial well of masterpieces to assemble changing exhibits. The building also houses the Architec-

ture and Design Center, with changing exhibits on those topics (www.arkdes.se, covered by a separate ticket). All of the exhibits are illuminated by an excellent, free audioguide that makes modern art meaningful to visitors who might not otherwise appreciate it (download the audioguide app using the museum's Wi-Fi).

Cost and Hours: Museum-120 kr, Architecture and Design Center-80 kr, 180 kr for both, free on Fri from 18:00; Tue and Fri 10:00-20:00, Wed-Thu and Sat-Sun 10:00-18:00, closed Mon; fine bookstore, harborview café, T-bana: Kungsträdgården plus 10-minute walk, or take bus #65, tel. 08/5202-3500, www.modernamuseet.se.

Östermalm

What this ritzy residential area lacks in museums, it makes up for in posh style. Explore its stately streets, dine in its destination restaurants, and be sure to explore the delightful, upscale Saluhall food market right on Östermalmstorg. Östermalm's harborfront is hemmed in by the pleasant park called Nybroplan; from here, ferries lead to various parts of the city and beyond (as this is the jumping-off point for cruises into Stockholm's archipelago). If connecting to the sights in Djurgården, consider doing Östermalm by foot.

Waterside Walk

Enjoy Stockholm's ever-expanding shoreline promenades. Tracing the downtown shoreline while dodging in-line skaters and ice-cream trolleys (rather than cars and buses), you can walk from Slussen across Gamla Stan, all the way to the good ship *Vasa* in Djurgården. Perhaps the best stretch is along the waterfront Strandvägen street (from Nybroplan past weather-beaten old boats and fancy facades to Djurgården). As you stroll, keep in mind that there's free fishing in central Stockholm, and the harbor waters are restocked every spring with thousands of new fish. Locals tell of one lucky lad who pulled in an 80-pound salmon. The waterside lanes are extremely bike-friendly here and throughout Stockholm.

Stockholm's Djurgården

DJURGÅRDSBRON

To Gärdet

To Nybroplan

STRANDVÄGEN   ÖSTERMALM

SJÖCAFÉET
(CAFÉ, BIKE RENTAL
& INFORMATION)

200 Meters

200 Yards

To Nybroplan   JUNIBACKEN

GALÄRVARVSVÄGEN

DJURGÅRDSVÄGEN

ROSENDALSVÄGEN

NORDIC
MUSEUM

VASA
MUSEUM

GALÄR
CEMETERY

WEST
ENTRY

BJÖRN
BJERGET

BJÖRN
BJORG

HARBOR
SHUTTLE
FERRIES

ESTONIA
MEMORIAL

SPIRIT
MUSEUM

HAZELIUSPORTEN

SKANSEN

MUSEUM OF
MODERN ART

MARITIME MUSEUM
BOAT HALL #2

PICNIC AREA,
FOLK DANCING

AQUARIUM

DJURGÅRDEN

WC

ABBA:
THE MUSEUM

OLD
TOWN

SKEPPS-
HOLMEN

ALLMÄNNA

GRÖNA
LUND
AMUSEMENT
PARK

SKANSEN
MAIN
ENTRANCE

ROLLDSBACKEN

DJURGÅRDSVÄGEN

Baltic
Sea

KASTELL-
HOLMEN

OAXEN SLIP
BISTRO

To Thielska Galleriet,
Rosendal's Garden &
Rosendal's Slott

To Gamla Stan
& Slussen

STOCKHOLM

DJURGÅRDEN

Four hundred years ago, Djurgården was the king's hunting ground (the name means "Animal Garden"). You'll see the royal gate to the island immediately after the bridge that connects it to the mainland. Now this entire lush island is Stockholm's fun center, protected as a national park. It still has a smattering of animal life among its biking paths, picnicking families, art galleries, various amusements, and museums, which are some of the best in Scandinavia.

Orientation: Of the three great sights on the island, the Vasa and Nordic museums are neighbors, and Skansen is a 10-minute walk away (or hop on any bus or tram—they come every couple of minutes). Several lesser or special-interest attractions (from the ABBA museum to an amusement park) are also nearby.

To get around more easily, consider **renting a bike** as you enter the island. You can get one at Sjöcaféet, a café just over the Djurgårdsbron bridge; they also rent boats (bikes-80 kr/hour, 275 kr/day; canoes-150 kr/hour, kayaks-125 kr/hour; open May-Oct daily 9:00-21:00, closed off-season and in bad weather; handy city cycle maps, tel. 08/660-5757, www.sjocafeet.se).

In the concrete building upstairs from the café, you'll find a **Djurgården visitors center,** with free maps, island bike routes, brochures, and information about the day's events (you can also buy ABBA museum tickets here; center open daily in summer 8:00-20:00, shorter hours off-season).

Getting There: Take tram #7 from Sergels Torg (the stop is right under the highway overpass) or Nybroplan (in front of the gilded theater building) and get off at one of these stops: Nordic Museum (used also for Vasa Museum), Liljevalc Gröna Lund (for ABBA museum), or Skansen. In summer, you can take a ferry from Nybroplan or Slussen (see "Getting Around Stockholm," earlier). Walkers enjoy the harborside Strandvägen promenade, which leads from Nybroplan directly to the island (described under "Waterside Walk," earlier).

Major Museums on Djurgården
▲▲▲Skansen

Founded in 1891, Skansen was the first in what became a Europe-wide movement to preserve traditional architecture in open-air museums. It's a huge park gather-ing more than 150 historic build-ings (homes, churches, shops, and schoolhouses) transplanted from all corners of Sweden. Other languages have borrowed the Swedish term "Skansen" (which originally meant "the Fort") to describe an "open-air museum." Today, tourists enjoy ex-ploring this Swedish-culture-on-a-

lazy-Susan, seeing folk crafts in action and wonderfully furnished old interiors. Kids love Skansen, where they can ride a life-size wooden *Dala*-horse and stare down a hedgehog, visit Lill-Skansen (a children's zoo), and take a mini-train or pony ride. While it's lively June through August before about 17:00, at other times of the year it can seem pretty dead; consider skipping it if you're here off-season.

Cost and Hours: 160 kr, kids-60 kr, less off-season; park open daily May-late-June 10:00-19:00, late-June-Aug 10:00-22:00, Sept 10:00-18:00, Oct and March-April 10:00-16:00, Nov-Feb 10:00-15:00; historical buildings generally open 11:00-17:00, late June-Aug some until 19:00, most closed in winter. Check their excel-lent website for "What's Happening at Skansen" during your visit (www.skansen.se) or call 08/442-8000 (press 1 for a live operator).

Music: Skansen does great music in summer. There's fiddling (30-minute performances June-Aug Tue-Fri at 18:15), folk dancing (June-Aug Tue-Fri at 19:00, also Sat-Sun at 16:00), and public danc-ing to live bands (Mon-Sat from

20:00, call for that evening's theme—big band, modern, ballroom, folk). Confirm performance times before you go.

Visiting Skansen: Skansen isn't designed as a one-way loop; it's a sprawling network of lanes and buildings, yours to explore.

For the full story, invest in the 75-kr museum guidebook. With the book, you'll understand each building you duck into and even learn about the Nordic animals awaiting you in the zoo. Check the live crafts schedule at the information stand by the main entrance to make a smart Skansen plan. Guides throughout the park are happy to answer your questions—but only if you ask them. The old houses come alive when you take the initiative to get information.

From the entrance, bear left to find the escalator, and ride it up to **"The Town Quarter"** (Stadskvarteren), where shoemakers, potters, and glass-blowers are busy doing their traditional thing (daily 10:00-17:00) in a re-created Old World Stockholm. Continuing deeper into the park—past the bakery, spice shop/grocery, hardware store, and a cute little courtyard café—you'll reach the central square, **Bollnäs-torget** (signed as "Central Skansen" but labeled on English maps as "Market Street"), with handy food stands. The rest of Sweden spreads out from here. Northern Swedish culture and architecture is in the north (top of park map), and southern Sweden's in the south (bottom of map). Various homesteads—each one clustered protectively around an inner courtyard—are scattered around the complex.

Poke around. Follow signs—or your instincts. It's worth stepping into the old, red-wood Seglora Church (just past Bollnästorget), which aches with atmosphere under painted beams. The park has two different zoos: Lill-Skansen is a children's petting zoo. Beyond the big brick spa tower and carnival rides sprawls the Scandinavian Animals section, with bears, wolves, moose ("elk"), seals, reindeer (near the Sami camp), and other animals.

Eating at Skansen: The park has ample eating options to suit every budget. The most memorable—and affordable—meals are at the small folk food court on the main square, **Bollnästorget.** Here, among the duck-filled lakes, frolicking families, and peacenik local toddlers who don't bump on the bumper cars, kiosks dish up "Sami slow food" (smoked reindeer), waffles, hot dogs, and more. There are lots of picnic benches—Skansen encourages **picnicking.** (A small grocery store is tucked away across the street and a bit to the left of the main entrance.)

STOCKHOLM

For a sit-down meal, the old-time **Stora Gungan Krog,** right at the top of the escalator in the craftsmen's quarter, is a cozy inn (100-180-kr indoor or outdoor lunches—meat, fish, or veggie— with a salad-and-cracker bar). Another snug spot is **Gubbhyllan,** on the ground floor and fine porch of an old house (90-kr sand- wiches, 130-160-kr meals, at base of escalator, just past main en- trance). For a less atmospheric choice, consider one of three restau- rants that share a modern building facing the grandstand (just up the hill inside the main entrance), all with nice views over the city: the simple **Skansen Terrassen** cafeteria (100-170-kr meals); **Tre Byttor Taverne,** with 18th-century pub ambience (140-kr lunches, 170-240-kr main courses); and, upstairs, the fussy **Solliden** res- taurant, with a dated blue-and-white dining hall facing a wall of windows; the main reason to eat here is the big *smörgåsbord* lunch (370 kr, served 12:00-16:00).

Aquarium: The "aquarium"—featuring lemurs, meerkats, ba- boons, Gila monsters, giant anacondas, rattlesnakes, geckos, croc- odiles, colorful tree frogs, and small sharks...but almost no fish—is located within Skansen, but is not covered by your Skansen ticket. Only animal lovers find it worth the steep admission price, but if you have a Stockholm Card, it's a fun and free walk-through (120 kr, Sept-May daily 10:00-16:00, tel. 08/660-1082, www.skansen- akvariet.se).

▲▲▲Vasa Museum (Vasamuseet)

Stockholm turned a titanic flop into one of Europe's great sight- seeing attractions. The glamorous but unseaworthy warship *Vasa*— top-heavy with an extra cannon deck—sank 40 minutes into her 1628 maiden voyage when a breeze caught the sails and blew her over. After 333 years at the bottom of Stockholm's harbor, she rose again from the deep with the help of marine archae- ologists. Rediscovered in 1956 and raised in 1961, this Edsel of the sea  is today the best-preserved ship of its age anywhere—housed since 1990 in a brilliant museum. The masts perched atop the roof—best seen from a distance—show the actual height of the ship.

Cost and Hours: 130 kr, includes film and tour; daily June- Aug 8:30-18:00; Sept-May 10:00-17:00 except Wed until 20:00; WCs on level 3, good café, Galärvarvet, Djurgården, tel. 08/5195- 4800, www.vasamuseet.se.

Getting There: The *Vasa* is on the waterfront immediately be- hind the stately brick Nordic Museum (described later), a 10-min- ute walk from Skansen. Or you can take tram #7 from downtown.

To get from the Nordic Museum to the Vasa Museum, face the Nordic Museum and walk around to the right (going left takes you into a big dead-end parking lot).

Crowd-Beating Tips: The museum can have very long lines, but they generally move quickly—you likely won't wait more than 15-20 minutes. If crowds are a concern, get here either right when it opens, or after about 16:00 (but note that the last tour starts at 16:30).

Tours: The free 25-minute **tour** is worthwhile. Because each guide is given license to cover whatever he or she likes, no two tours are alike—if you're fascinated by the place, consider taking two different tours to pick up new details. In summer, English tours run on the hour and half-hour (last tour at 16:30); off-season (Sept-May) tours go 3/day Mon-Fri, hourly Sat-Sun (last tour at 15:30). Listen for the loudspeaker announcement, or check at the info desk for the next tour. Alternatively, you can access the **audioguide** by logging onto the museum's Wi-Fi (www.vasamuseet.se/audioguide).

Film: The excellent 17-minute film digitally re-creates *Vasa*-era Stockholm (and the colorfully painted ship itself), dramatizes its sinking, and documents the modern-day excavation and preservation of the vessel. It generally runs three times per hour; virtually all showings are either in English or with English subtitles.

Visiting the Museum: For a thorough visit, plan on spending at least an hour and a half—watch the film, take a guided tour, and

linger over the exhibits (this works in any order). After buying your ticket, head inside. Sort out your film and tour options at the information desk to your right.

Upon entry, you're prow-to-prow with the great ship. The ***Vasa,*** while not quite the biggest ship in the world when launched in 1628, had the most firepower, with two fearsome decks of cannons. The 500 carved wooden statues draping the ship—once painted in bright colors—are all symbolic of the king's power. The 10-foot lion on the magnificent prow is a reminder that Europe considered the Swedish King Gustavus Adolphus the "Lion from the North." With this great ship, Sweden was preparing to establish its empire and become more engaged in European power politics. Specifically, the Swedes (who already controlled much of today's Finland and Estonia) wanted to push south to dominate the whole of the Baltic Sea, in order to challenge their powerful rival, Poland.

Designed by a Dutch shipbuilder, the *Vasa* had 72 guns of the same size and type (a rarity on mix-and-match warships of the age), allowing maximum efficiency in reloading—since there was no need to keep track of different ammunition. Unfortunately, the king's unbending demands to build it high (172 feet tall) but skinny made it extremely unstable; no amount of ballast could weigh the ship down enough to prevent it from tipping.

Now explore the **exhibits,** which are situated on six levels around the grand hall, circling the ship itself. All displays are well described in English. You'll learn about the ship's rules (bread can't be older than eight years), why it sank (heavy bread?), how it's preserved (the ship, not the bread), and so on. Best of all is the chance to do slow laps around the magnificent vessel at different levels. Now painstakingly restored, 98 percent of the *Vasa*'s wood is original (modern bits are the brighter and smoother planks).

On **level 4** (the entrance level), right next to the ship, you'll see a 1:10 scale model of the *Vasa* in its prime—vividly painted and fully rigged with sails. Farther along, models show how the *Vasa* was salvaged; a colorful children's section re-creates the time period; and a 10-minute multimedia show explains why the *Vasa* sank (alternating between English and Swedish showings). Heading behind the ship, you'll enjoy a great view of the sculpture-slathered stern of the *Vasa.* The facing wall features full-size replicas of the carvings, demonstrating how the ship was originally colorfully painted.

Several engaging displays are on **level 5.** "Life On Board" lets you walk through the gun deck and study cutaway models of the hive of activity that hummed below decks (handy, since you can't enter the actual ship). Artifacts—including clothes actually worn by the sailors—were salvaged along with the ship. "Battle!" is a small exhibit of cannons and an explanation of naval warfare.

Level 6 features "The Sailing Ship," with models demonstrating how the *Vasa* and similar vessels actually sailed. You'll see the (very scant) remains of some of the *Vasa*'s actual riggings and sails. **Level 7** gives you even higher views over the ship.

Don't miss **level 2**—all the way at the bottom (ride the handy industrial-size elevator)—with some of the most interesting exhibits. "The Shipyard" explains how this massive and majestic vessel was brought into being using wood from tranquil Swedish forests. Tucked under the ship's prow is a laboratory where today's scientists continue with their preservation efforts. The "Objects" exhibit shows off actual items found in the shipwreck, while "Face to Face" introduces you to some of those who perished when the

Vasa sunk—with faces that were re-created from skeletal remains. Nearby, you'll see some of the skeletons found in the shipwreck.

As you exit, you'll pass a hall of (generally excellent) temporary exhibits.

▲▲Nordic Museum (Nordiska Museet)

Built to look like a Danish Renaissance palace, this museum offers a fascinating peek at 500 years of traditional Swedish lifestyles. The exhibits insightfully place everyday items into their social/historical context in ways that help you really grasp various chapters of Sweden's past. It's arguably more informative than Skansen. Take time to let the excellent, included audioguide enliven the exhibits.

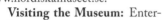

Cost and Hours: 100 kr, free Wed after 17:00 Sept-May; daily 10:00-17:00, Wed until 20:00 Sept-May; Djurgårdsvägen 6-16, at Djurgårdsbron, tram #7 from downtown, tel. 08/5195-6000, www.nordiskamuseet.se.

Visiting the Museum: Entering the museum's main hall, you'll be face-to-face with Carl Milles' huge painted-wood statue of Gustav Vasa, father of modern Sweden. The rest of this floor is usually devoted to temporary exhibits.

Highlights of the permanent collection are on the top two floors. Head up the stairs, or take the elevator just to the left of

Gustav. Begin on floor 4 and work your way down.

On **floor 4,** four different exhibits ring the grand atrium. The "Homes and Interiors" section displays 400 years of home decor. As you travel through time—from dark, heavily draped historical rooms to modern living rooms, and from rustic countryside cottages to aristocratic state bedrooms—you'll learn the subtle meaning behind everyday furniture that we take for granted. For example, the advent of television didn't just change entertainment—it gave people a reason to gather each evening in the living room, which, in turn, became a more-used (and less formal) part of people's homes. You'll learn about the Swedish designers who, in the 1930s, eschewed stiff-backed traditional chairs in favor of sleek perches that merged ergonomics and looks—giving birth to functionalism.

Also on this floor, the "Folk Art" section shows off colorfully painted furniture and wood carvings; vibrant traditional costumes; and rustic Bible-story illustrations that adorned the walls of peasants' homes. The "Sápmi" exhibit tells the fascinating and often overlooked story of the indigenous Sami people (formerly called "Lapps"), who lived in the northern reaches of Norway, Sweden, Finland, and Russia centuries before Europeans created those modern nations. On display are shoes, ceremonial knives, colorful hats and clothing, and other features of Sami culture. You'll learn how their nomadic lifestyle—following their herds of grazing reindeer—allowed them to survive so far north, and how the Sami (who still number around 20,000) have had an impact on greater Swedish society. Finally, tucked behind the stairwell, the "Small Things" collection shows off timepieces, ceramics, and tobacco pipes, among other items.

Floor 3 has several smaller exhibits. The most interesting are "Table Settings" (with carefully set tables from the last century, representing different time periods, social classes, and occasions—from an elegant tea party to a rowdy pub) and "Traditions" (showing and describing each old-time celebration of the Swedish year—from Christmas to Midsummer—as well as funerals, confirmations, and other life events). Also on display: 300 years of Swedish clothing illustrating how we define ourselves through our attire; jewelry and textile exhibits; a dollhouse and toy collection; and a photo exhibition pulled from the museum's archive.

▲ABBA: The Museum

The Swedish pop group ABBA was, for a time, a bigger business than Volvo. After bursting on the scene in 1974 by winning the Eurovision Song Contest with "Waterloo," and increasing their fame by serenading Sweden's newly minted queen with "Dancing Queen" in 1976, they've sold more than 380 million records, and the musical based on their many hits, *Mamma Mia!*, has been enjoyed by 50 million people. It was only a matter of time before Stockholm opened an ABBA museum, which is conveniently located just across the street from Skansen and next to Gröna Lund amusement park. Like everything ABBA, it is aggressively for-profit and slickly promoted, with the steepest ticket price in town (not covered by Stockholm Card). True to its subject, it's bombastic, glitzy, and highly interactive. If you like ABBA, it's lots of fun; if you love ABBA, it's ▲▲▲ nirvana.

Cost and Hours: 195 kr, 500-kr family ticket covers two adults and up to four kids, cash not accepted, daily 10:00-20:00, shorter hours off-season—likely until 18:00, Djurgårdsvägen 68, bus #44 or tram #7 to Liljevalc Gröna Lund stop, tel. 08/1213-2860, www.abbathemuseum.com.

Audioguide: ABBA aficionados will happily fork over 40 kr extra for the intimate audioguide, in which Agnetha, Benny, Björn, and Anni-Frid share their memories, in their own words.

Getting In: To control the crowds, only 75 people are let in every 15 minutes with timed-entry tickets. The museum strongly encourages getting tickets in advance from their website or at the TI. In fact, they'll charge you 20 kr extra per ticket to book one in person (but computer terminals are standing by if you want to "pre-book" on the spot). It can be crowded on summer weekends, in which case you may have to wait for a later time.

Visiting the Museum: The museum is high-tech, with plenty of actual ABBA artifacts, re-created rooms where the group did its composing and recording (including their famous "Polar Studio" and their rustic archipelago cottage), a room full of gold and platinum records, plenty of high-waisted sequined pantsuits, and lots of high-energy video screens. Everything is explained in English.

Included in the ticket is a "digital key" that lets you take advantage of several interactive stations. For example, you can record a music video karaoke-style as a fifth member of the group—with virtual ABBA members dancing around you—and pick up the production from their website. A small wing features the Swedish Music Hall of Fame, but apart from that, it's all ABBA.

Waterfront Sights

While the tram zips sightseers between the Vasa Museum and Skansen, it's a short, enjoyable, and very scenic walk along the waterfront—a delight on a nice day. You'll see food stands, boats bobbing in the harbor, and sunbathing Swedes.

You'll also pass several sights. Between the Vasa Museum and the Djurgårdsbron bridge is **Junibacken,** a fairy-tale house based on the writings of Astrid Lindgren, who created *Pippi Longstocking*. While oriented toward Swedish kids, American children may enjoy it, too (entry fee, www.junibacken.se). The pier directly in front of the Vasa Museum is actually part of the **Maritime Museum** (Sjöhistoriska), where historic ships are moored (typically big icebreakers from the Arctic, and sometimes military boats). Farther south, near the amusement park, is the Maritime Museum's boat hall #2 (Båthall 2), filled with more boats and exhibits (free entry to all Maritime Museum sights, www.sjohistoriska.se). And halfway along the waterfront is the following odd but endearing museum that offers a weird but welcome break from heavier sightseeing.

Spiritmuseum

The museum's highly conceptual permanent exhibit considers the role of alcohol—and specifically, flavored vodkas—in Swedish society. While Sweden got a reputation for its "loose morals" in the 1970s (mostly surrounding sex and nudity), at the same time it was extremely puritanical when it came to alcohol; the government actively tried to get Swedes to stop drinking (hence the liquor-store system and sky-high alcohol taxes that still exist). In the exhibit's season-themed rooms, you'll be able to smell different types of flavored liquors (orange in the spring, elderflower in the summer, and so on); upstairs, you can ace a virtual pub quiz, recline (or nap) in the boozy drunk-simulator room, and step into a garishly lit, buzzing room that simulates a hangover. The temporary exhibits here are also quite good.

Cost and Hours: 100 kr, 200-kr ticket adds a taster kit of flavored vodkas; daily June-Aug 10:00-18:00, Sept-May 10:00-17:00, Tue until 20:00 year-round, Djurgårdsvägen 38, tel. 08/1213-1300, www.spritmuseum.se.

Other Djurgården Sights

Gröna Lund Amusement Park

Stockholm's venerable and lowbrow Tivoli-type amusement park still packs in the local families and teens on cheap dates. It's a busy venue for local pop concerts.

Cost and Hours: 110 kr, late April-late Sept daily 12:00-23:00, closed off-season, www.gronalund.com.

▲Thielska Galleriet

If you liked the Larsson and Zorn art in the National Gallery, and/or if you're a Munch fan, this charming mansion on the water at the far end of the Djurgården park is worth the trip.

Cost and Hours: 100 kr, Tue-Sun 12:00-17:00, closed Mon, bus #69 (not #69K) from downtown, tel. 08/662-5884, www.thielska-galleriet.se.

▲Biking the Garden Island

In all of Stockholm, Djurgården is the most natural place to enjoy a bike ride. There's a good and reasonably priced bike-rental place just over the bridge as you enter the island, and a world of park-like paths and lanes with harbor vistas to enjoy.

Ask for a free map and route tips when you rent your bike. Figure about an hour to pedal around Djurgården's waterfront perimeter; it's mostly flat, but with some short, steeper stretches that take you up and

over the middle of the island. Those who venture beyond the Skansen park find themselves nearly all alone in the lush and evocative environs.

At the summit of the island you'll come upon Rosendal's Garden, with a bakery and café (daily 11:00-17:00). You can sit in the greenhouse or in the delightful orchard or flower garden, where locals come to pick a bouquet and pay by the weight. (The garden is fertilized by the horse pies from adjacent Skansen.) Just beyond is the **Rosendals Slott,** the cute mini-palace of Karl Johans XIV, founder of the Bernadotte dynasty. This palace, in the so-called Karl Johans style ("Empire style"), went together in prefabricated sections in the 1820s. The story is told on a board in front, and a 9-ton porphyry vase graces the backyard.

A garden café at the eastern tip of the island offers a scenic break midway through your pedal. For a longer ride, you can cross the canal to the Ladugårdsgärdet peninsula ("Gärdet" for short), a swanky, wooded residential district just to the north.

SÖDERMALM

Just south of Gamla Stan, the Södermalm district is the downscale antidote to the upscale, ritzy areas where most tourists spend their time (Norrmalm, Östermalm, Djurgården, and Gamla Stan). Södermalm recently has been in vogue thanks to Stieg Larsson's *Girl with the Dragon Tattoo* novels, in which Lisbeth Salander and her cohorts represent the "real," hardscrabble Stockholm (all the villains come from the posh north side). While the area has few tourist sights (aside from the Stockholm City Museum, which is closed for renovation through 2017), it offers fine views and is a fun place to eat. Towering over Södermalm's main road is the Skrapan building, with the Himlen view terrace on its 25th floor. The big white sphere on the horizon is the Ericsson Globe, a hockey arena.

With newfound popularity comes investment, and Södermalm is gentrifying quickly—giving it something of a split personality. While the often-repeated comparison to "Stockholm's Brooklyn" is a stretch (this relatively sterile area lacks the loosey-goosey hipster charm of many such neighborhoods in the US and other parts of Europe), it does have a nice variety of shops, squares, restaurants, and bars where locals outnumber tourists. The most interesting areas to explore are along Götgatan and the zone south of Folkungagatan street—nicknamed "SoFo."

Getting There: To stroll this area, simply head from Gamla Stan through the confusing Slussen transit mess. Facing the big P-hus Slussen tunnel, turn right one block into the pedestrian area (uphill, passing the T-bana station on your left and the Stockholm City Museum on your right), then left onto colorful Götgatan, and head on up the hill. Alternatively, you can ride the T-bana to Medborgarplatsen, which puts you right on the area's main market square (but misses the interesting shops along Götgatan). Medborgarplatsen itself is a wonderful workaday plaza that feels like the center of a big urban neighborhood. Ringed by fun eateries, it's great for people-watching.

STOCKHOLM

ON THE OUTSKIRTS

The home and garden of Carl Milles, Sweden's greatest sculptor, is less than an hour from the city center. For sights farther outside Stockholm (all reachable by public transportation), see the next chapter.

▲Millesgården

The villa and garden of Carl Milles is a veritable forest of statues by Sweden's greatest sculptor. Millesgården is dramatically situated on

a bluff overlooking the harbor in Stockholm's upper-class suburb of Lidingö. While the art is engaging and enjoyable, even the curators have little to say about it from an interpretive point of view—so your visit is basically without guidance. But in Milles' house, which dates from the 1920s, you can see his north-lit studio and get a sense of his creative genius.

Carl Milles spent much of his career teaching at the Cranbrook Academy of Art in Michigan. But he's buried here at his villa, where he lived and worked for 20 years, lovingly designing this sculpture garden for the public. Milles wanted his art to be displayed on pedestals...to be seen "as if silhouettes against the sky." His subjects—often Greek mythological figures such as Pegasus or Poseidon—stand out as if the sky was a blank paper. Yet unlike silhouettes, Milles' images can be enjoyed from many angles. And Milles liked to enliven his sculptures by incorporating water features into his figures. *Hand of God,* perhaps his most famous work, gives insight into Milles' belief that when the artist created, he was—in a way—divinely inspired.

Cost and Hours: 100 kr; daily 11:00-17:00 except closed Mon in Oct-April; English booklet explains the art, restaurant and café, tel. 08/446-7590, www.millesgarden.se.

Getting There: Catch the T-bana to Ropsten, then take bus #207 to within a five-minute walk of the museum; several other #200-series buses also get you close enough to walk (allow about 45 minutes total each way).

Shopping in Stockholm

Sweden offers a world of shopping temptations. Smaller stores are open weekdays 10:00-18:00, Saturdays until 17:00, and Sundays 11:00-16:00. Some of the bigger stores (such as NK, H&M, and Åhléns) are open later on Saturdays and Sundays.

Fun Chain Stores

These chains have multiple branches around town.

DesignTorget, dedicated to contemporary Swedish design, receives a commission for selling the unique works of local designers (generally Mon-Fri 10:00-19:00, Sat 10:00-18:00, Sun 11:00-17:00, big branch underneath Sergels Torg—enter from basement level of Kulturhuset, other branches are at Nybrogatan 23 and at the airport, www.designtorget.se).

Systembolaget is Sweden's state-run liquor store chain. A sample of each bottle of wine or liquor sits in a display case. A card in front explains how it tastes and suggests menu pairings. Look for the item number and order at the counter. Branches are in Hötorget underneath the movie theater complex, in Norrmalm at Vasagatan 21, and just up from Östermalmstorgat Nybrogatan 47 (Mon-Wed 10:00-18:00, Thu-Fri 10:00-19:00, Sat 10:00-15:00, closed Sun, www.systembolaget.se).

Hamngatan

The main shopping zone between Kungsträdgården and Sergels Torg has plenty of huge department stores. At the top of Kungsträdgården, **Illums Bolighus** is a Danish design shop. Across the street, **Nordiska Kompaniet** (NK) is elegant and stately; the Swedish design (downstairs) and kitchenware sections are particularly impressive. The classy **Gallerian** mall is just up the street from NK and stretches seductively nearly to Sergels Torg. The **Åhléns** store, kitty-corner across Sergels Torg, is less expensive than NK and has two cafeterias and a supermarket. Affordable clothing chain **H&M** has a store right across the street.

Mood Stockholm

The city's most exclusive mall is a downtown block filled with big-name Swedish and international designers, plus a pricey food court and restaurants. The preciously upscale decor and mellow music give it a Beverly Hills vibe (Mon-Fri 10:00-20:00, Sat 10:00-18:00, Sun 11:00-17:00, Regeringsgatan 48). This mall anchors a ritzy, pedestrianized shopping zone; for additional trendy and exclusive shops, browse the nearby streets Jakobsbergsgatan and Biblioteksgatan.

Södermalm

When Swedes want the latest items by local designers, they skip the downtown malls and head for funky Södermalm. **Götgatan,** the main drag that leads from Slussen up to this neighborhood, is a particularly good choice, with shop after shop of mostly Swedish designers. Boutiques along here—some of them one-offs, others belonging to Swedish chains—include Weekday (jeans and dressed-up casual), Filippa K (smart casual and business attire), and Tiogruppen (bold bags and fabrics).

Nybrogatan

This short and pleasant traffic-free street, which connects Östermalmstorg with the Nybroplan waterfront, is lined with small branches of interesting design shops, including Nordiska Galleriet (eye-catching modern furniture, at #11), DesignTorget (described earlier, at #16), and Hemslöjden (Swedish handicrafts, at #23). It also has shoe and handbag stores, and an enticing cheese shop and bakery.

Flea Markets

For a *smörgåsbord* of Scanjunk, visit the **Loppmarknaden,** northern Europe's biggest flea market, at Vårberg Center (free entry weekdays and Sat-Sun after 15:00, 15 kr on weekends—when it's busiest; open Mon-Fri 11:00-18:00, Sat 10:00-16:00, Sun 11:00-16:00; T-bana: Vårberg, tel. 08/710-0060, www.loppmarknaden. se). Hötorget, the produce market, also hosts a Sunday flea market in summer.

Nightlife and Entertainment in Stockholm

Bars and Music in Gamla Stan

The street called Stora Nygatan, with several lively bars, has perhaps the most accessible and reliable place for live jazz in town: Stampen. Several pubs here offer live Irish traditional music sessions or bluegrass several times each week; they tend to share musicians, who sometimes gather at one of these pubs for impromptu jam sessions (ask around, or stroll this street with your ears peeled). While it may seem odd to listen to Irish or bluegrass music in Stockholm, these venues are extremely popular with locals.

Stampen Jazz & Rhythm 'n' Blues Pub has two venues under one roof: a stone-vaulted cellar below and a fun-loving saloon-like bar upstairs (check out the old instruments and antiques hanging from the ceiling). From Monday through Thursday, there's live music in the saloon. On Friday and Saturday, bands alternate sets in both the saloon and the cellar (160-kr cover Fri-Sat only, open

Mon-Thu 17:00-late, Fri-Sun 20:00-late, special free jam session Sat 14:00-18:00, Stora Nygatan 5, tel. 08/205-793, www.stampen. se).

Several other lively spots are within a couple of blocks of Stampen on Stora Nygatan. Your options include **Wirströms Pub** (live blues bands play in crowded cellar Tue-Sat 21:00-24:00, no cover, 62-kr beers, open daily 11:00-late, Stora Nygatan 13, www. wirstromspub.se); **O'Connells Irish Pub** (a lively expat sports bar with music—usually Tue-Sat at 21:00, open daily 12:00-late, Stora Nygatan 21, www.oconnells.se); and **The Liffey** (classic Irish pub with 150-180-kr pub grub, live music Wed and Fri-Sun at 21:30, open daily 11:00-late, Stora Nygatan 40-42, www.theliffey.se).

Icebar Stockholm

If you just want to put on a heavy coat and gloves and drink a fancy vodka in a modern-day igloo, consider the fun, if touristy,

 Icebar Stockholm. Everything's ice—shipped down from Sweden's far north. The bar, the glasses, even the tip jar are made of ice. You get your choice of vodka drinks and 45 minutes to enjoy the scene (on-line booking-185 kr, drop-ins pay 10 kr more—on weekends drop-ins only allowed after 21:45, additional drinks-95 kr, reservations smart; daily June-Aug 11:15-24:00, Sept-May 15:00-24:00; in the Nordic C Hotel adjacent to the main train station's Arlanda Express platform at Vasaplan 4, tel. 08/5056-3124, www.icebarstockholm.se). If you go too early, it can be really dead—you'll be all alone. At busy times, people are let in all at once every 45 minutes. That means there's a long line for drinks, and the place goes from being very crowded to almost empty as people gradually melt away. At first everyone's just snapping photos. While there are ice bars all over Europe now, this is the second one (after the Ice Hotel in Lapland). And it really is pretty cool...a steady 23°F.

Cinema

In Sweden, international movies are shown in their original language with Swedish subtitles. Swedish theaters sometimes charge more for longer films, and tickets come with assigned seats (drop by to choose seats and buy a ticket, box offices generally open 11:00-22:00 daily). The Hötorget and Drottninggatan neighborhoods have many theaters.

Swedish Massage, Spa, and Sauna

To treat yourself to a Swedish spa experience—maybe with an authentic "Swedish massage"—head for the elegant circa-1900 **CentralBadet Spa.** It's along downtown's main strolling street, Drottninggatan, tucked back inside a tranquil and inviting garden courtyard. Admission includes entry to an extensive gym, "bubblepool," sauna, steam room, "herbal/crystal sauna," and an elegant Art Nouveau pool. Most areas are mixed, with men and women together, but some areas are reserved for women. If you won't make it to Finland, enjoy a sauna here. Bring your towel into the sauna—not for modesty, but for hygiene (to separate your body from the bench). The steam room is mixed; bring two towels (one for modesty and the other to sit on). The pool is more for floating than for jumping and splashing. The leafy courtyard restaurant is a relaxing place to enjoy affordable, healthy, and light meals (220 kr, increases to 320 kr on Sat, towels and robes available for rent; slippers are required—20 kr to buy, 10 kr to rent; open Mon-Fri 7:00-20:30, Sat 9:00-20:30, Sun 9:00-17:30, last entry one hour before closing, ages 18 and up, Drottninggatan 88, 10 minutes up from Sergels Torg, tel. 08/5452-1300, reservation tel. 08/218-821, www.centralbadet.se).

Sleeping in Stockholm

Between business travelers and the tourist trade, demand for Stockholm's hotels is healthy but unpredictable, and most hotels' rates vary from day to day. For each hotel (for comparison's sake), I've listed the average price for a standard double room in high season (mid-June-mid-Aug)—but your rate will almost certainly be higher or lower, depending on the timing of your visit. Use my descriptions to determine which hotels interest you, then check the specific rates online; it's easiest to do this on a comparison booking site (but once you see the rates, book directly with the hotel, which may net you a lower price).

A program called **Destination Stockholm** is, for many (especially families), the best way to book a big hotel on weekends or during the summer. When you reserve a hotel room through this service, it includes a free Stockholm à la Carte card, which covers public transportation, most major sights, and lots of tours for the duration of your visit (even better than the Stockholm Card). Kids sleep free (and also get the card). Reserve by phone or online; be sure to review the cancellation policy before you commit (tel. 08/663-0080, www.destination-stockholm.com).

Consider hostels. Stockholm's hostels are among Europe's best, offering good beds in simple but interesting places for about

Sleep Code

Abbreviations   (7 kr = about $1, country code: 46, area code: 08)
S = Single, **D** = Double/Twin, **T** = Triple, **Q** = Quad, **b** = bathroom
Price Rankings
  $$$ Higher Priced—Most rooms 1,800 kr or more
   $$ Moderately Priced—Most rooms 800-1,800 kr
    $ Lower Priced—Most rooms 800 kr or less
Unless otherwise noted, English is spoken, credit cards are accepted, breakfast is included, and Wi-Fi is generally free. Prices change; verify current rates online or by email. For the best prices, always book directly with the hotel.

300 kr per night for a dorm bed. Each has helpful English-speaking staff, pleasant family rooms, and good facilities.

NEAR THE TRAIN STATION

$$$ Freys Hotel is a Scan-mod, four-star place, with 127 compact, smartly designed rooms. It's well-situated for train travelers, located on a dead-end pedestrian street across from the central station. While big, it works hard to be friendly and welcoming. Its cool, candlelit breakfast room becomes a bar in the evening, popular for its selection of Belgian microbrews (Sb-1,750 kr, Db-2,470 kr, check website for specials as low as Db-1,750 kr, air-con, guest computer, Wi-Fi, Bryggargatan 12, tel. 08/5062-1300, www. freyshotels.com, freys@freyshotels.com).

$$$ Scandic Kungsgatan, central but characterless, fills the top floors of a downsized department store with 270 rooms. If the Starship *Enterprise* had a low-end hotel, this would be it. Save about 100 kr by taking a "cabin" room with no windows—the same size as other rooms, quiet, and well-ventilated (Db-2,000 kr, air-con, guest computer, Wi-Fi, Kungsgatan 47, tel. 08/723-7220, www.scandichotels.com, kungsgatan@scandichotels.com).

$$ HTL Kungsgatan, jamming modernity into a classic old building a few blocks from the station, takes a futuristic approach to providing just what travelers really need—and nothing else. You reserve online, then check in at a self-service kiosk on arrival. Roving receptionists are standing by in the coffee bar for any needs. The 274 rooms are small and functional (no desk or chairs) but trendy and comfortable. Everything surrounds a stylish, glassy atrium boasting a hip lounge/restaurant with a youthful party vibe and live music until 24:00 on most weekends (Sb/Db-1,700 kr, can be much lower—around 700 kr—in slow times, 100 kr less for windowless but well-ventilated "sleeper" room, breakfast-75 kr,

STOCKHOLM

STOCKHOLM

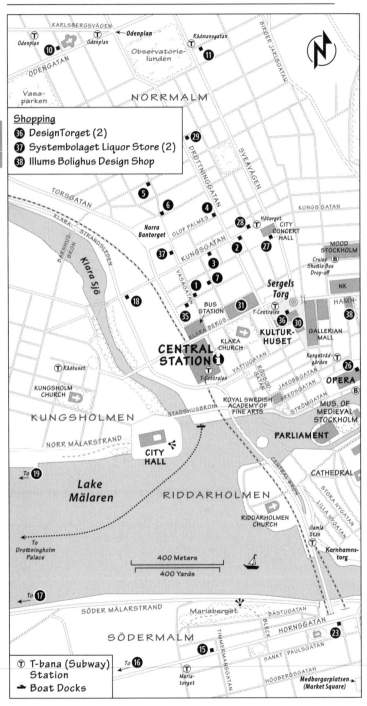

Shopping
36 DesignTorget (2)
37 Systembolaget Liquor Store (2)
38 Illums Bolighus Design Shop

T-bana (Subway) Station
Boat Docks

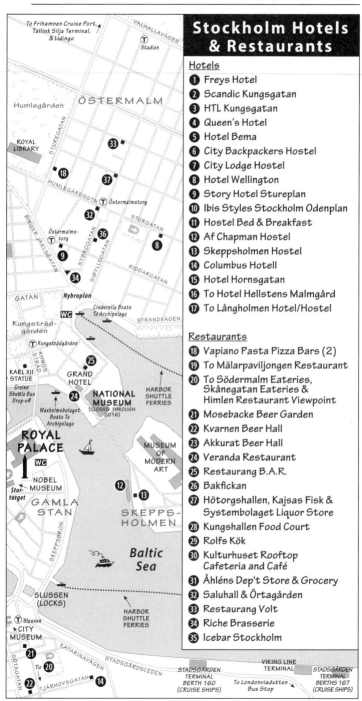

STOCKHOLM

Stockholm Hotels & Restaurants

Hotels

1. Freys Hotel
2. Scandic Kungsgatan
3. HTL Kungsgatan
4. Queen's Hotel
5. Hotel Bema
6. City Backpackers Hostel
7. City Lodge Hostel
8. Hotel Wellington
9. Story Hotel Stureplan
10. Ibis Styles Stockholm Odenplan
11. Hostel Bed & Breakfast
12. Af Chapman Hostel
13. Skeppsholmen Hostel
14. Columbus Hotell
15. Hotel Hornsgatan
16. To Hotel Hellstens Malmgård
17. To Långholmen Hotel/Hostel

Restaurants

18. Vapiano Pasta Pizza Bars (2)
19. To Mälarpaviljongen Restaurant
20. To Södermalm Eateries, Skånegatan Eateries & Himlen Restaurant Viewpoint
21. Mosebacke Beer Garden
22. Kvarnen Beer Hall
23. Akkurat Beer Hall
24. Veranda Restaurant
25. Restaurang B.A.R.
26. Bakfickan
27. Hötorgshallen, Kajsas Fisk & Systembolaget Liquor Store
28. Kungshallen Food Court
29. Rolfs Kök
30. Kulturhuset Rooftop Cafeteria and Café
31. Åhléns Dep't Store & Grocery
32. Saluhall & Örtagården
33. Restaurang Volt
34. Riche Brasserie
35. Icebar Stockholm

air-con, elevator, Wi-Fi, Kungsgatan 53, tel. 08/4108-4150, www. htlhotels.com, htlkungsgatan@htlhotels.com).

$$ Queen's Hotel enjoys a great location at the quiet top end of Stockholm's main pedestrian shopping street (about a 10-minute walk from the train station, or 15 minutes from Gamla Stan). The 59 rooms are well worn, but reasonably priced for the convenient location. Rooms facing the courtyard are quieter (Sb-1,100 kr, Db-1,300 kr, bigger "superior" Db with pull-out sofa bed-1,900, 10 percent discount for readers who book direct—ask for it; if booking online enter rate code "RICKS" in all caps, extra bed-250 kr, elevator, guest computer, Wi-Fi, Drottninggatan 71A, tel. 08/249-460, www.queenshotel.se, info@queenshotel.se).

$$ Hotel Bema, a bit farther out than the others listed in this section, is a humble place that rents 12 fine rooms for some of the best prices in town (S-900 kr, Db-1,100 kr, extra person-250 kr, breakfast served at nearby café, bus #65 from station to Upplandsgatan 13—near the top of the Drottninggatan pedestrian street, or walk about 15 minutes from the train station—exit toward *Vasagatan* and head straight up that street, tel. 08/232-675, www. hotelbema.se, info@hotelbema.se).

$ City Backpackers, with 140 beds a quarter-mile from the station, is youthful but classy (bunk in 8- to 12-bed room-230 kr, in 6-bed room-290 kr, in 4-bed room-320 kr; bunk-bed D-740 kr, 40 percent more for Fri- or Sat-night stay without weeknight; sheets-25 kr, free cook-it-yourself pasta, breakfast-55 kr, pay laundry, guest computer, Wi-Fi, movies, tours, sauna, lockers, Upplandsgatan 2A, tel. 08/206-920, www.citybackpackers.se, info@ citybackpackers.se).

$ City Lodge Hostel, on a quiet side street just a block from the central train station, has 68 beds, a convivial lounge, and a kitchen with free cooking staples (bunk in 18-bed dorm-220 kr, in 6-bed dorm-275 kr, in quad-315 kr; a few tiny bunk-bed doubles-640 kr, bigger D-820 kr, cheaper outside of summer; sheets-50 kr, breakfast-60-kr, guest computer, Wi-Fi, laundry, no curfew, Klara Norra Kyrkogata 15, tel. 08/226-630, www.citylodge.se, info@citylodge.se).

IN QUIETER RESIDENTIAL AREAS

These options in Norrmalm and Östermalm are in stately, elegant neighborhoods of five- and six-story turn-of-the-century apartment buildings. All are too long of a walk from the station with luggage, but still in easy reach of downtown sights and close to T-bana stops.

$$$ Hotel Wellington, two blocks off Östermalmstorg, is in a less handy but charming part of town. It's modern and bright, with hardwood floors, 60 rooms, and a friendly welcome. While it may seem pricey, it's a cut above in comfort, and its great amenities—such as a very generous buffet breakfast, free coffee all day long, and free buffet dinner in the evening—add up to a good value (prices range widely, but in summer generally Db-1,820 kr, smaller Db for 200 kr less, mention this book when you book direct for a 10 percent discount, guest computer, Wi-Fi, free sauna, old-fashioned English bar, garden terrace bar, T-bana: Östermalmstorg, exit to Storgatan and walk past big church to Storgatan 6; tel. 08/667-0910, www.wellington.se, cc.wellington@choice.se).

$$$ Story Hotel Stureplan is a colorful boutique hotel with a creative hipster vibe. Conveniently located near a trendy dining zone between Östermalmstorg and the Nybroplan waterfront, it has 83 rooms above a sprawling, cleverly decorated, affordably priced restaurant. You'll book online, check yourself in at the kiosk, and receive a text message with your door key code (tight bunk-bed Db-1,700 kr, standard Db-2,000 kr, more for bigger rooms, elevator, free minibar drinks, Wi-Fi, Riddargatan 6, tel. 08/5450-3940, www.storyhotels.com).

$$$ Ibis Styles Stockholm Odenplan rents 76 cookie-cutter rooms on several floors of a late-19th-century apartment building (Db-1,950 kr, about 300 kr cheaper with nonrefundable "advance saver" rate, Wi-Fi, T-bana: Odenplan, Västmannagatan 61, reservation tel. 08/1209-0000, reception tel. 08/1209-0300, www.ibisstyles.se, odenplan@uniquehotels.se).

$ Hostel Bed and Breakfast is a tiny, woody, and easygoing independent hostel renting 36 beds in various dorm-style rooms. Many families stay here (bed in 4-bed room-320 kr, Sb-550 kr, Db-780 kr, sheets-50 kr, kitchen, laundry, Wi-Fi, across the street from T-bana: Rådmansgatan, just off Sveavägen at Rehnsgatan 21, tel. 08/152-838, www.hostelbedandbreakfast.com, info@hostelbedandbreakfast.com).

IN GAMLA STAN

These options are in the midst of sightseeing, a short bus or taxi ride from the train station.

$$$ Scandic Gamla Stan offers Old World elegance in the heart of Gamla Stan (a 5-minute walk from Gamla Stan T-bana station). Its 52 small rooms are filled with chandeliers and hardwood floors (Sb-1,400 kr, Db-2,000 kr, 200 kr extra for larger room, elevator, Wi-Fi, Lilla Nygatan 25, tel. 08/723-7250, www.scandichotels.com, gamlastan@scandichotels.com).

$$$ Lady Hamilton Hotel, classic and romantic, is shoehorned into Gamla Stan on a quiet street a block below the cathedral and Royal Palace. The centuries-old building has 34 small but plush and colorfully decorated rooms. Each one is named for a Swedish flower and is filled with antiques (Db-2,200 kr, a few hundred kronor more for a bigger "corner" room with a better view, elevator, guest computer, Wi-Fi, Storkyrkobrinken 5, tel. 08/5064-0100, www.ladyhamiltonhotel.se, info@ladyhamiltonhotel.se).

$$ Urban Hostel Old Town is a sane and modern hostel conveniently located in an untrampled part of Gamla Stan, just a few steps off the harbor. Conscientiously run, with 135 beds in small but tidy modern rooms, it's not a party hostel—grown-ups will feel comfortable here (bunk in 16-bed dorm-295 kr, S-695 kr, D-900 kr, Db-1,500 kr, T-1,100 kr, Q-1,400 kr, Qb-2,200 kr, breakfast-75 kr, air-con, elevator, Wi-Fi, Nygränd 5, tel. 08/1214-0444, www.urbanhostels.se, info@urbanhostels.se).

$$ The Ånedin Hostel is a floating hotel, moored near the foot of the Royal Palace. Once a cruise boat, the classic liner MS *Birger Jarl* has 130 cabins, varying from small simple rooms to superior cabins with private baths (Db-600 kr, Qb-900 kr, prices vary by size of room and berth configuration, breakfast-90 kr, Wi-Fi in public spaces, Skeppsbron Tullhus 1, tel. 08/6841-0130, www.anedinhostel.com, info@anedinhostel.com).

ON SKEPPSHOLMEN

This relaxing island—while surrounded by Stockholm—feels a world apart, both in terms of its peacefulness and its somewhat less convenient transportation connections (you'll rely on bus #65, the shuttle ferry, or your feet—it's about a 20-minute walk from the train station).

$ Af Chapman Hostel, a permanently moored 100-year-old schooner, is Europe's most famous youth hostel and has provided a berth for the backpacking crowd for years. Renovated from keel to stern, the old salt offers 120 bunks in four- to six-bed rooms (bunk-375 kr, D-850 kr, fancier "navigational" or "captain's" cabins-1,240 kr/1,030 kr, 50 kr less for members, Wi-Fi, see next listing for contact information). Reception and breakfast are at the Skeppsholmen Hostel (next).

$ Skeppsholmen Hostel, just ashore from the *Af Chapman*, has 160 beds (bunk in 17-bed dorm-265 kr, in 3- to 6-bed room-310 kr, D-690 kr, 50 kr less for members; includes sheets, breakfast-80 kr, laundry service, no lockout, Wi-Fi, tel. 08/463-2266, chapman@stfturist.se).

ON OR NEAR SÖDERMALM

Södermalm is residential and hip, with Stockholm's best café and bar scene. You'll need to take the bus or T-bana to get here from the train station.

$$$ Columbus Hotell—located in a 19th-century building that formerly housed a brewery, a jail, and a hospital—has 69 quiet rooms facing a big courtyard in the heart of Södermalm (Sb-1,600 kr, Db-1,850 kr, Tb-2,100 kr, rates may increase with planned renovation—which may also add an elevator; T-bana: Medborgarplatsen or bus #53 from train station to Tjärhovsplan, then a 5-minute walk to Tjärhovsgatan 11; tel. 08/5031-1200, www.columbushotell.se, info@columbushotell.se).

$$ Hotel Hornsgatan is a tidy, welcoming, nicely decorated B&B upstairs in an old townhouse facing a busy but elegant-feeling boulevard. Four of the 17 small rooms have private baths; the others share five modern bathrooms. Thoughtfully run by Clara and Scott, this is a good value for the location (S-900 kr, Sb-1,300 kr, D-1,100 kr, Db-1,500 kr, elevator, Wi-Fi, reception staffed until 22:00—make arrangements if arriving late, Hornsgatan 66B, T-bana: Mariatorget plus a short walk, 15-minute walk from Slussen/Gamla Stan, tel. 08/658-2901, www.hotelhornsgatan.se, info@hotelhornsgatan.se).

$$ Hotel Hellstens Malmgård is an eclectic collage of 50 rooms crammed with antiques in a circa-1770 mansion. No two rooms are alike, but all have modern baths and quirky touches such as porcelain stoves or four-poster beds. Unwind in its secluded cobblestone courtyard, and you may forget what century you're in (Db-1,600 kr, elevator, Wi-Fi; T-bana: Zinkensdamm, then a 5-minute walk to Brännkyrkagatan 110; tel. 08/4650-5800, www.hellstensmalmgard.se, hotel@hellstensmalmgard.se).

$$ Långholmen Hotel/Hostel is on Långholmen, a small island off Södermalm that was transformed in the 1980s from Stockholm's main prison into a lovely park. Rooms are converted cells in the old prison building. You can choose between hostel- and hotel-standard rooms at many different price levels (hostel rooms: dorm bed-260 kr, bunk-bed twin D-630 kr, Db-750 kr, Tb-900 kr, Q-1,040 kr, Qb-1,160 kr, 50 kr less for members, sheets-65 kr, breakfast-98 kr; hotel rooms: Db-2,050 kr, extra bed-250 kr, includes breakfast, about 100 kr cheaper for nonrefundable booking, Wi-Fi, laundry room, kitchen, cafeteria, free parking, on-site swimming; T-bana: Hornstull, walk 10 minutes down and cross small bridge to Långholmen island, follow hotel signs 5 minutes farther; tel. 08/720-8500, www.langholmen.com, hotel@langholmen.com).

Eating in Stockholm

To save money, eat your main meal at lunch, when cafés and restaurants have 95-kr daily special plates called *dagens rätt* (generally Mon-Fri only). Most museums have handy cafés (with lots of turnover and therefore fresh food, 100-kr lunch deals, and often with fine views). Convenience stores serve gas station-style food (and often have seats). As anywhere, department stores and malls are eager to feed shoppers and can be a good, efficient choice. If you want culturally appropriate fast food, stop by a local hot dog stand. Picnics are a great option—especially for dinner, when restaurant prices are highest. There are plenty of park-like, harborside spots to give your cheap picnic some class. I've also listed a few splurges—destination restaurants that offer a good sample of modern Swedish cooking.

IN GAMLA STAN

Most restaurants in Gamla Stan serve the 95-kr weekday lunch special mentioned above, which comes with a main dish, small salad, bread, and tap water. Choose from Swedish, Asian, or Italian cuisine. Several popular places are right on the main square (Stortorget) and near the cathedral. Järntorget, at the far end, is another fun tables-in-the-square scene. Touristy places line Västerlånggatan. You'll find more romantic spots hiding on side lanes. I've listed my favorites below (for locations, see the adjacent map).

Grillska Huset is a cheap and handy cafeteria run by Stockholms Stadsmission, a charitable organization helping the poor. It's grandly situated right on the old square, with indoor and outdoor seating (tranquil garden up the stairs and out back), fine daily specials, a hearty salad bar, and a staff committed to helping others. You can feed the hungry (that's you) and help house the homeless at the same time. The 95-kr daily special gets you a hot plate, salad, and coffee, or choose the 90-kr salad bar—both available Mon-Fri 11:00-14:00 (also 100-kr meals, café serves sandwiches and salads daily 10:00-18:00, Stortorget 3, tel. 08/787-8605). They also have a fine little bakery *(brödbutik)* with lots of tempting cakes and pastries (30-40-kr premade sandwiches, closed Sun).

Kryp In, a small, cozy restaurant (the name means "hide away") tucked into a peaceful lane, has a stylish hardwood and candlelit interior, great sidewalk seating, and an open kitchen letting you in on Vladimir's artistry. If you dine well in Stockholm once (or twice), I'd do it here. It's gourmet without pretense. They serve delicious, modern Swedish cuisine with a 475-kr three-course dinner. In the good-weather months, they serve weekend lunches, with specials starting at 120 kr. Reserve ahead for dinner (200-290-kr plates, daily 17:00-23:00, May-Oct Sat-Sun from 12:30, a block off Stortorget at Prästgatan 17, tel. 08/208-841, www.restaurangkrypin.se).

STOCKHOLM

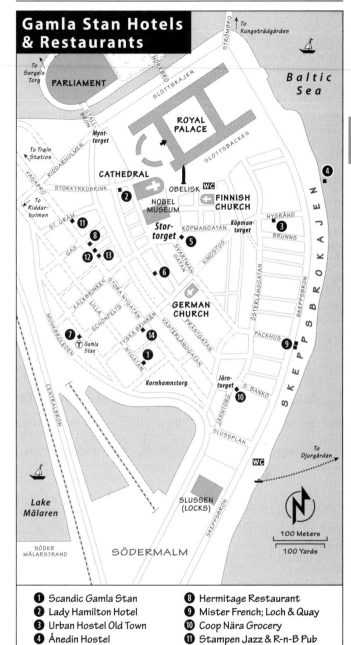

Gamla Stan Hotels & Restaurants

To Kungsträdgården

To Sergels Torg

PARLIAMENT

STRÖMBRO

NORRBRO

SLOTTSKAJEN

Baltic Sea

STÄLL-BRON

ROYAL PALACE

Mynt-torget

SLOTTSBACKEN

To Train Station

RIDDARHOLMEN

VASABRO

CATHEDRAL

STORKYRKOBRINK

OBELISK

WC

FINNISH CHURCH

NYGRÄND

To Riddarholmen

ST. GRÄM.

NOBEL MUSEUM

Stor-torget

KÖPMANGATAN

Köpman-torget

BRUNNS

GAS.

KÅCKBRINKEN

STORA NYGATAN

SVARTMAN-GATAN

KINDSTUG

SKEPPSBRON

ÖSTERLÄNGGATAN

GERMAN CHURCH

LILLA

SCHÖNFELIS

TYSKA BRINKEN

VÄSTERLÅNGGATAN

PRÄSTGATAN

PACKHUS

SKEPPSBROKAJEN

Gamla Stan

NYGATAN

Kornhamnstorg

Järn-torget

JÄRNTORG.

S. BANKO

To Djurgården

CENTRALBRON

SLUSSPLAN

WC

Lake Mälaren

SLUSSEN (LOCKS)

SKEPPSBRON

N

100 Meters

100 Yards

SÖDER MÄLARSTRAND

SÖDERMALM

❶ Scandic Gamla Stan
❷ Lady Hamilton Hotel
❸ Urban Hostel Old Town
❹ Ånedin Hostel
❺ Grillska Huset Cafeteria
❻ Kryp In Restaurant
❼ Vapiano Pasta Pizza Bar

❽ Hermitage Restaurant
❾ Mister French; Loch & Quay
❿ Coop Nära Grocery
⓫ Stampen Jazz & R-n-B Pub
⓬ Wirströms Pub
⓭ O'Connells Irish Pub
⓮ The Liffey Irish Pub

Vapiano Pasta Pizza Bar, a bright, high-energy, family-oriented eatery, issues you an electronic card as you enter. Circulate to the different stations, ordering up whatever you like as they swipe your card (80-150-kr pastas, pizzas, and salads). Portions are huge and easily splittable. As you leave, your card indicates the bill. Season things by picking a leaf of basil or rosemary from the potted plant on your table. Because tables are often shared, this a great place for solo travelers (daily 11:00-24:00, right next to entrance to Gamla Stan T-bana station, Munkbrogatan 8, tel. 08/222-940). They also have locations on Östermalm (facing Humlegården park at Sturegatan 12) and Norrmalm (between the train station and Kungsholmen at Kungsbron 15).

Hermitage Restaurant is a friendly, faded, hippie-feeling joint that serves a tasty vegetarian buffet in a warm communal dining setting (120 kr gets you a meal, Mon-Fri 11:00-21:00, Sat-Sun 12:00-21:00, Stora Nygatan 11, tel. 08/411-9500).

Picnic Supplies in Gamla Stan: The handy and affordable **Coop Nära** mini supermarket is strategically located on Järntorget, at the Slussen end of Gamla Stan; the **Munkbrohallen** supermarket downstairs in the Gamla Stan T-bana station is also very picnic-friendly (both open daily 7:00-22:00).

DINING ON THE WATER

In Gamla Stan: The harbor embankment of Gamla Stan, facing a gorgeous Stockholm panorama, is lined with swanky quayside eateries and al fresco tables. While prices are high, the setting is memorably romantic—sophisticated, yet waterfront-casual. The listings below are open daily 11:30-24:00 in good weather, when it's smart to call ahead to reserve a view table.

Mister French is the classiest option, with French and American cuisine and a sleek black-and-white color scheme. Choose between the bar (200-kr simple bar food) or the full restaurant (200-300-kr main courses, cheaper half-portions available). They serve a 150-kr lunch special. While the brasserie interior is classy, I'd eat here only for the outdoor views (Tullhus 2, tel. 08/202-095, www.mrfrench.se).

Loch & Quay, next door, is a simpler "summer pub" with lower prices (160-220-kr pub grub, 120-150-kr lunches available until 14:30, Tullhus 2, tel. 08/225-755).

In Kungsholmen, Behind City Hall: On a balmy summer's eve, **Mälarpaviljongen** is a dreamy spot with hundreds of locals enjoying the perfect lakefront scene, as twinkling glasses of rosé shine like convivial lanterns. From City Hall, walk 15 minutes along Lake Mälaren (a treat in itself) and you'll find a hundred casual outdoor tables on a floating restaurant and among the trees on shore. Line up at the cafeteria to order a drink, snack, or com-

Swedish Cuisine

Most people don't travel to Sweden for the food. Though potatoes and heavy sauces are a focus of the country's cuisine, its variety of meat and fish dishes can be surprisingly satisfying. If you don't think you'll like Swedish or Scandinavian food, be sure to splurge at a good-quality place before you pass final judgment.

Every region of Sweden serves different specialties, but you'll always find *svenska köttbullar* on the menu (Swedish meatballs made from beef and pork in a creamy sauce). This Swedish favorite is topped with lingonberry jam, which is served with many meat dishes across Scandinavia. Potatoes, seemingly the only vegetable known to Sweden, make for hearty *kroppkakor* dumplings filled with onions and minced meat. The northern variation, *pitepalt*, is filled with pork. Southern Sweden takes credit for *pytt i panna*, a medley of leftover meat and diced potatoes that's fried and served with an egg yolk on top. And it seems that virtually every meal you'll eat here includes a side of boiled, small new potatoes.

Though your meals will never be short on starch, be sure to try Sweden's most popular baked good, *kanelbulle*, for a not-so-light snack during the day. This pastry resembles a cinnamon roll, but it's made with cardamom and topped with pearl sugar. Enjoy one during *fika*, the daily Swedish coffee break so institutionalized that many locals use the term as a verb (see page 27).

Like those of its Nordic neighbors, Sweden's extensive coastline produces some of the best seafood in the world. A light, tasty appetizer is *gravad lax*, a dill-cured salmon on brown bread or crackers. You'll also likely encounter *Toast Skagen*. This appetizer-spread is made from shrimp, dill, mayonnaise, and Dijon mustard, and is eaten on buttered toast.

For a main course, the most popular seafood dish is crayfish. Though eaten only by the aristocracy in the 16th century, these shellfish have since become a nationwide delicacy; they're cooked in brine with dill and eaten cold as a finger food. Traditional crayfish parties take place outdoors on summer evenings, particularly in August. Friends and family gather around to indulge in this specialty with rye bread and a strong cheese. The Swedes also love Baltic herring; try *stekt strömming*, a specialty of the east coast, which is herring fried with butter and parsley. As usual, it's served with potatoes and lingonberry jam. Adventurous diners can have their herring pickled or fermented—or order more unusual dishes like reindeer.

As for beer, the Swedes classify theirs by alcohol content. The higher the number, the higher the alcohol content—and the price. *Klass 1* is light beer—very low-alcohol. *Klass 2* is stronger, but still mild. And *Klass 3* has the most body, the most alcohol, and the highest price.

plete meal. When it's cool, they have heaters and blankets. The walk along the lake back into town caps the experience beautifully (60-kr beer, 130-kr cocktails, 110-kr lunch plates, 180-240-kr evening meals, open in good weather April-Sept daily 11:00-late, easy lakeside walk or T-bana to Fridhemsplan plus a 5-minute walk to Nörr Mälarstrand 63, no reservations, tel. 08/650-8701).

In Djurgården: **Sjöcaféet,** beautifully situated and greedily soaking up the afternoon sun, fills a woody terrace stretching along the harbor just over the Djurgårdsbron bridge. In summer, this is a fine place for a meal or just a drink before or after your Skansen or *Vasa* visit. They have affordable lunch plates (105 kr, Mon-Fri 11:00-13:00 only); after 14:00, you'll pay 130-180 kr per plate (also 12-kr pizzas, order at the bar, daily 8:00-20:00, often later in summer, closed off-season, tel. 08/661-4488).

Oaxen Slip Bistro, a trendy harborfront place 200 yards below the main Skansen gate, serves creative Nordic cuisine with sturdy local ingredients in a sleek interior or on its delightfully woody terrace. Overlooking a canal in what feels like an old shipyard, and filled with in-the-know locals, this place is a real treat. Reservations are smart (200-kr plates, game and seafood, daily 12:00-14:00 & 17:00-21:30, Beckholmsvägen 26, tel. 08/5515-3105, www.oaxen.com).

Dinner Cruises on Lake Mälaren: The big sightseeing company Strömma sells a variety of lunch and dinner cruises that allow you to enjoy the delightful waterways of Stockholm and the archipelago while you eat. Options include shorter dinner cruises to Drottningholm Palace (2.5 hours round-trip), longer ones to the outer archipelago (up to 5 hours), and *smörgåsbord* cruises around Lake Mälaren. For prices, details, and booking, check www.stromma.se; see also their other options, including a shrimp cruise and a jazz cruise.

SÖDERMALM STREETS AND EATS

This quickly gentrifying, working-class district, just south of Gamla Stan (steeply uphill from Slussen), has some of Stockholm's most enticing food options—especially for beer lovers. It's also a bit less swanky, and therefore more affordable, than many of the city's more touristy neighborhoods. Combine dinner here with a stroll through a side of Stockholm many visitors miss.

Götgatan and Medborgarplatsen

The neighborhood's liveliest street is the artery called Götgatan, which leads from Slussen (where Södermalm meets Gamla Stan) steeply up into the heart of Södermalm. Here, mixed between the boutiques, you'll find cafés tempting you to join the Swedish coffee break called *fika*, plus plenty of other eateries. Even if you don't dine in Södermalm, it's worth a stroll here just for the window-shopping fun.

At the top of the street, you'll pop out into the big square called Medborgarplatsen. This neighborhood hang-out is a great scene, with almost no tourists and lots of options—especially for Swedish fast food. (My favorite, Melanders Fisk, is listed next.) Outdoor restaurant and café tables fill the square, which is fronted by a big food hall. (There's also a T-bana stop here for an easy return home after dinner.) The recommended Kvarnen beer hall (see later) is just around the corner to the left.

Melanders Fisk, facing the square, has only outside tables (and is therefore an option only in warm weather). You order at the bar and join locals in this classic scene. *Skagenröra*, shrimp with mayo on toast or filling a baked potato, is the signature dish—and dear to the Swedish heart (115 kr; also 90-kr lunch plates daily, 130-150-kr fish plates served daily until 21:00, after 21:00 it's only *skagenröra*, Medborgarplatsen 3, tel. 08/644-4040).

Skånegatan and Nytorget

A bit farther south, these cross-streets make another good spot to browse among fun and enticing restaurants, particularly for ethnic cuisine.

Nytorget Urban Deli is the epitome of Södermalm's trendy-hipster vibe and an amazing scene. It's half fancy artisanal deli-catessen—with all manner of ingredients—and half white-sub-way-tile-trendy eatery, with indoor and outdoor tables filled with Stockholm yuppies eating well. If it's busy—as it often is—they'll scrawl your name at the bottom of the long butcher-paper waiting list (no reservations). If it's full, you can grab a place at the bar and eat there (international and Swedish modern dishes, 100-190-kr light meals, 190-225-kr bigger meals, daily 8:00-23:00, at the far end of Skånegatan at Nytorget 4, tel. 08/5990-9180).

Nytorget Urban Deli Picnic: The upscale grocery store attached to the deli seems designed for picnickers, with lots of creative boxed meals and salads to go (same address and hours—see listing above). The park across the street has lots of benches and picnic tables.

Kohphangan, with an almost laughably over-the-top island atmosphere that belies its surprisingly good Thai food, has been a hit for 20 years. (Thailand is to Swedes what Mexico is to Americans—the sunny "south of the border" playground.) The ambience? Mix a shipwreck, Bob Marley, and a Christmas tree and you've got it (160-220-kr dishes, daily 12:00-24:00, Skånegatan 57, tel. 08/642-5040).

Gossip is a mellow, unpretentious hole-in-the-wall serving Bangladeshi street food (120-160-kr dishes, Mon-Fri 11:00-23:00, Sat-Sun 13:00-23:00, Skånegatan 71, tel. 08/640-6901).

Beer and Pub Grub in Södermalm

Södermalm cultivates the most interesting beer scene in this beer-crazy city.

Beer Garden with a View: **Mosebacke,** perched high above town, is a gravelly beer garden with a grand harbor view. The beer garden (open only on warm summer evenings) prides itself on its beer rather than its basic grub (read: bar snacks). It's a good place to mix with a relaxed young crowd. As each of the beer kiosks has its own specialties, survey all of them before making your choice (a block inland from the top of the Katarina viewing platform, look for the triumphal arch at Mosebacke Torg 3, tel. 08/556-09890, www.sodrateatern.com). The adjacent restaurant serves fine 250-kr plates.

Classic Swedish Beer Halls: Two different but equally traditional Södermalm beer halls serve well-executed, hearty Swedish grub in big, high-ceilinged, orange-tiled spaces with rustic wooden tables.

Kvarnen ("The Mill") is a reliable choice with a 1908 ambience. As it's the home bar for the supporters of a football club, it can be rough. Pick a classic Swedish dish from their fun and easy menu (100-130-kr starters, 140-200-kr main courses, daily 17:00-24:00, Tjärhovsgatan 4, tel. 08/643-0380).

Pelikan, an old-school beer hall, is less sloppy and has nicer food. It's a bit deeper into Södermalm (120-230-kr starters, 190-270-kr main courses, Mon-Thu 16:00-23:00, Fri-Sun 13:00-23:00, Blekingegatan 40, tel. 08/5560-9290).

Trendier "Craft Beer" Pub: **Akkurat** has a staggering variety of microbrews—both Swedish and international (on tap and bottled)—as well as whisky. It's great if you wish you were in England with a bunch of Swedes (short menu of 190-240-kr pub grub, Mon-Fri 11:00-24:00, Sat 15:00-24:00, Sun 18:00-24:00, Hornsgatan 18, tel. 08/644-0015).

IN NORRMALM
At or near the Grand Hotel

Royal Smörgåsbord: To stuff yourself with all the traditional Swedish specialties (a dozen kinds of herring, salmon, reindeer, meatballs, lingonberries, and shrimp, followed by a fine table of cheeses and desserts) with a super harbor view, consider splurging at the Grand Hotel's dressy **Veranda Restaurant.** While very touristy, this is considered the finest *smörgåsbord* in town. The Grand Hotel, where royal guests and Nobel Prize winners stay, faces the harbor across from the palace. Pick up their English flier for a good explanation of the proper way to enjoy this grand buffet. Reservations are often necessary (485 kr in evening, 445 kr for lunch, drinks extra, open nightly 18:00-22:00, also open for lunch Sat-Sun

13:00-16:00 year-round and Mon-Fri 12:00-15:00 in May-Sept, no shorts after 18:00, Södra Blasieholmshamnen 8, tel. 08/679-3586, www.grandhotel.se)

Restaurang B.A.R. has a fun energy, with diners surveying the meat and fish at the ice-filled counter, talking things over with the chef, and then choosing a slab. Prices are on the board, and everything's grilled (250-300-kr meals, open daily except closed Sun-Mon in July, behind the Grand Hotel at Blasieholmsgatan 4, tel. 08/611-5335).

At the Royal Opera House

The Operakällaren, one of Stockholm's most exclusive restaurants, runs a little "hip pocket" restaurant called **Bakfickan** on the side, specializing in traditional Swedish quality cooking at reasonable prices. It's ideal for someone eating out alone, or for anyone wanting an early dinner. Choose from two different daily specials or pay 180-280 kr for main dishes from their regular menu (160-180-kr specials served daily from 12:00 until they run out—which can be early or as late as 20:00, no specials in July). Sit inside—at tiny private side tables or at the big counter with the locals—or, in good weather, grab a table on the sidewalk, facing a cheery red church (Mon-Sat 12:00-22:00, closed Sun, on the inland side of Royal Opera House, tel. 08/676-5809).

At or near Hötorget

Hötorget ("Hay Market"), a vibrant outdoor produce market just two blocks from Sergels Torg, is a fun place to picnic-shop. The outdoor market closes at 18:00, and many merchants put their unsold produce on the push list (earlier closing and more desperate merchants on Sat).

Hötorgshallen, next to Hötorget (in the basement under the modern cinema complex), is a colorful indoor food market with an old-fashioned bustle, plenty of exotic and ethnic edibles, and—in the tradition of food markets all over Europe—some great little eateries (Mon-Fri 10:00-18:00, Sat 10:00-15:00, closed Sun). The best is **Kajsas Fisk,** hiding behind the fish stalls. They serve delicious fish soup to little Olivers who can hardly believe they're getting... more. For 95 kr, you get a big bowl of hearty soup, a simple salad, bread and crackers—plus one soup refill. Their *stekt strömming* (traditional fried herring and potato dish) is a favorite (90-150-kr daily fish specials, Mon-Fri 11:00-18:00, Sat 11:00-16:00, closed Sun, Hötorgshallen 3, tel. 08/207-262). There's a great kebab and falafel place a few stalls away.

Kungshallen, an 800-seat indoor food court across the square from Hötorget, has more than a dozen eateries. The main floor is a bit more upscale, with sit-down places and higher prices, while the basement is a shopping-mall-style array of fast-food counters, including Chinese, sushi, pizza, Greek, and Mexican. This is a handy place to comparison-shop for a meal at lower prices (Mon-Fri 9:00-22:00, Sat-Sun 12:00-22:00).

On or near Drottninggatan

The pleasant, pedestrianized shopping street called Drottninggatan, which runs from the train station area up into Stockholm's suburbs, is a fine place to find a forgettable meal but with memorable people-watching. Several interchangeable eateries with sidewalk tables line the street (and don't miss the delightful, leafy park courtyard of Centralbadet, at #88, with several outdoor cafés). None of them merits a special detour, except the next listing.

Rolfs Kök, a vibrant neighborhood favorite, is worth the pleasant five-minute stroll up from the end of Drottninggatan. The long bar up front fades into an open kitchen hemmed in with happy diners at counters, and tight tables fill the rest of the space before spilling out onto the sidewalk. Trendy, casual, and inviting, this bistro features international fare with a focus on Swedish classics and a good wine list. Reservations are smart (100-160-kr starters, 220-300-kr main courses, Mon-Fri 11:30-24:00, Sat-Sun 17:00-24:00, closed in July and sometimes early Aug—confirm it's open before making the trip, Tegnérgatan 41, tel. 08/101-696, www.rolfskok.se).

Near Sergels Torg

Kulturhuset Rooftop Eateries: Two places (one cheap and the other trendy) are handy for simple meals with great city views. **Cafeteria Panorama,** offering cheap eats and a salad bar, has both inside and outside seating with jaw-dropping vistas (90-kr lunch specials with salad bar, Sat-Mon 11:00-18:00, Tue-Fri 11:00-20:00). The more stylish **Mat and Bar café** has a pleasant garden setting with pricier food (daily until 21:00).

The many modern shopping malls and department stores around Sergels Torg all have appealing, if pricey, eateries catering to the needs of hungry local shoppers. **Åhléns** department store has a Hemköp supermarket in the basement (daily until 21:00) and two restaurants upstairs with 80-110-kr daily lunch specials (Mon-Fri 11:00-19:30, Sat 11:00-18:30, Sun 11:00-17:30).

IN ÖSTERMALM

Saluhall, on Östermalmstorg (near recommended Hotel Wellington), is a great old-time indoor market with top-quality artisanal producers and a variety of sit-down and takeout eateries. While it's nowhere near "cheap," it's one of the most pleasant market halls I've

seen, oozing with upscale yet traditional Swedish class. Inside you'll find Middle Eastern fare, sushi, classic Scandinavian open-face sandwiches, seafood salads, healthy wraps, cheese counters, designer chocolates, gourmet coffee stands, and a pair of classic old sit-down eateries (Elmqvist and Tystamare). This is your chance to pull up a stool at a lunch counter next to well-heeled Swedish yuppies (Mon-Thu 9:30-18:00, Fri until 19:00, Sat until 16:00, closed Sun).

Örtagården, upstairs from the Saluhall, is primarily a vegetarian restaurant and serves a 145-kr buffet weekdays until 17:00 and a larger 155-kr buffet evenings and weekends (Mon-Fri 11:00-22:00, Sat-Sun 11:00-21:00, entrance on side of market building at Nybrogatan 31, tel. 08/662-1728).

Restaurang Volt is a destination restaurant for foodies looking to splurge on "New Nordic" cooking: fresh, locally sourced ingredients fused into bold new recipes with fundamentally Swedish flavors. Owners Fredrik Johnsson and Peter Andersson fill their minimalist black dining room with just 31 seats, so reservations are essential (550 kr/four courses, 700 kr/six courses, no à la carte, Tue-Sat 18:00-24:00, closed Sun-Mon, Kommendörsgatan 16, tel. 08/662-3400, www.restaurangvolt.se).

Riche, a Parisian-style brasserie just a few steps off Nybroplan at Östermalm's waterfront, is a high-energy environment with a youthful sophistication. They serve up pricey but elegantly executed Swedish and international dishes in their winter garden, bright dining room, and white-tile-and-wine-glass-chandeliered bar (140-230-kr starters, 200-340-kr main courses, 175-kr plat du jour, Mon-Fri 7:30-24:00, Sat-Sun 12:00-24:00, Birger Jarlsgatan 4, tel. 08/5450-3560).

Stockholm Connections

BY BUS

Unless you have a rail pass, long-distance buses are cheaper than trains, such as from Stockholm to Oslo or Kalmar. Buses usually take longer, but have more predictable pricing, shorter ticket lines, and student discounts. Swebus is the largest operator (tel. 0771-21-8218, www.swebus.se); Nettbuss also has lots of routes (www.nettbuss.se). Some bus companies offer discounts with advance purchase.

From Stockholm by Bus to: Copenhagen (about 3/day with

change in Malmö, 9.5 hours, longer for overnight trips), **Oslo** (3/day, 8 hours), **Kalmar** (4/day, fewer on weekends, 6 hours).

BY TRAIN

The easiest and cheapest way to book train tickets is online at www.sj.se. Simply select your journey and pay for it with a credit card.
When you arrive at the train station, print out your tickets at a self-service ticket kiosk (bring your purchase confirmation code). You can also buy tickets at a ticket window in a train station, but this comes with long lines and a 5 percent surcharge. For timetables and prices, check online, call 0771/757-575, or use one of the self-service ticket kiosks.

As with airline tickets and hotel rooms, Swedish train ticket prices vary with demand. The cheapest are advance-purchase, nonchangeable, and nonrefundable.

For rail-pass holders, seat reservations are required on express (such as the "SJ high-speed" class) and overnight trains, and they're recommended on some longer routes (to Oslo, for example). Second-class seat reservations to Copenhagen cost 65 kr (150 kr in first class). If you have a rail pass, make your seat reservation at a ticket window in a train station, by phone (at the number above), or online (under "Buy Tickets," choose "pass 2cl" from the "customer card" menu).

From Stockholm by Train to: Uppsala (4/hour, 40 minutes; also possible on slower suburban *pendeltåg*—2/hour, 55 minutes, covered by local transit pass plus small supplement), **Växjö** (every 2 hours, 3.5 hours, change in Alvesta, reservations required), **Kalmar** (hourly, 4.5-5 hours, transfer in Alvesta, reservations required), **Copenhagen** (almost hourly, 5-6 hours on high-speed train, some with a transfer at Lund or Hässleholm, reservations required; overnight train requires a change in Malmö or Lund; all trains stop at Copenhagen airport before terminating at the central train station), **Oslo** (2/day direct Intercity trains, 6 hours; 2/day with change, 6-7.5 hours).

BY OVERNIGHT BOAT

Ferry boat companies run shuttle buses from the train station to coincide with each departure; check for details when you buy your ticket. When comparing prices between boats and planes, remember that the boat fare includes a night's lodging.

From Stockholm to: Helsinki and **Tallinn** (daily/nightly boats, 16 hours), **Turku** (daily/nightly boats, 11 hours). St. Peter Line connects Stockholm to **St. Petersburg,** but the trip takes two nights—you'll sail the first night to Tallinn, then a second night to St. Petersburg; returning, you'll sail the first night to Helsinki, and the second night to Stockholm (www.stpeterline.com). Note: To visit Russia, American and Canadian citizens need a visa (arrange weeks in advance).

BY CRUISE SHIP

For many more details on Stockholm's ports, and other cruise destinations, pick up my *Rick Steves Northern European Cruise Ports* guidebook.

Stockholm has two cruise ports: the more central **Stadsgården** port, used mainly by ships that are just passing through, is in Södermalm; the **Frihamnen** port, used primarily by ships that are beginning or ending a cruise, is three miles northeast of the city center.

Getting Downtown: Most cruise lines offer a convenient **shuttle bus** (about 100 kr round-trip) that drops you in downtown Stockholm near the Opera House. From there it's an easy walk or public bus/tram ride to various points of interest. It's not a bad value in this expensive city, where a single one-way ticket on public transit costs over $5. **Taxis** from each port are also available (depending on your destination, figure 115-190 kr from Stadsgården and 150-235 kr from Frihamnen). Other options, including a hop-on, hop-off bus or boat from Stadsgården or the public from Frihamnen, are explained next.

Port Details: TI kiosks (with bus tickets, city guides, and maps) open at both ports when ships arrive.

Stadsgården is a long embankment, with cruises arriving at areas that flank the busy Viking Line Terminal (used by boats to Helsinki). The nearest transportation hub (with bus and T-bana stops) is Slussen, which sits beneath the bridge connecting the Old Town/Gamla Stan and the Södermalm neighborhood. Berth 160 is an easy 10-minute **walk** to Slussen; berths 165/167 are farther out but still walkable (about 25 minutes to Slussen).

From Stadsgården, a good option is the handy **hop-on, hop-off harbor boat** tour, which departs from right next to the cruise dock and connects several worthwhile downtown areas for a reasonable price (120-160 kr for 24 hours, tickets often discounted from cruise port). A taxi stand is next to the TI kiosk just outside the port gate. Near the taxi stand is the departure point for **hop-on, hop-off tour buses**. The public bus from Stadsgården is not a convenient option.

Frihamnen is a sprawling, drab industrial port zone used by cruise liners as well as overnight Baltic boats. Cruises typically use one of three berths—634, 638, or 650. Berth 638 is the main dock and has the only dedicated terminal building (with a TI desk and gift shops). Along the main harborfront road you'll find a TI kiosk; hop-on, hop-off bus tours (pricey but convenient); and a public **bus** stop—a good option. Bus #76 zips you to several major sights, including Djurgårdsbron, Nybroplan, Kungsträdgården, Räntmästartrappan, and Slussen (4-7/hour Mon-Fri, 2-3/hour Sat, none on Sun). On weekends, you may be better off taking the less convenient but more frequent bus #1, which cuts across the top of Östermalm and Norrmalm to the train station (runs daily). You can't buy bus tickets on board—get one at the TI inside the terminal, at the booth near the bus stop, or from the ticket machine at the bus stop.

BY PLANE

For information on arriving at Stockholm's airports, see "Arrival in Stockholm," earlier in this chapter.

To Helsinki and Tallinn: Many low-fare airlines are offering flights across the Baltic. For flights from Stockholm to Helsinki, check www.flysas.com/fi; to Tallinn, also visit www.norwegian.com and www.estonian-air.com.

ROUTE TIPS FOR DRIVERS

Stockholm to Oslo: It's an eight-hour drive from Stockholm to Oslo. **Årjäng,** just before the Norwegian border, is a good place for a rest stop. At the border, change money at the little TI kiosk (on right side). Pick up the Oslo map and *What's On in Oslo,* and consider buying your Oslo Card here.

NEAR STOCKHOLM

Drottningholm Palace • Sigtuna • Uppsala

At Stockholm's doorstep is a variety of fine side-trip options—all within an hour of the capital. Drottningholm Palace, on the city's outskirts, was the summer residence—and most opulent castle—of the Swedish royal family, and has a uniquely well-preserved Baroque theater, to boot. The adorable town of Sigtuna is a cutesy, cobbled escape from the big city, studded with history and rune stones. Uppsala is Sweden's answer to Oxford, offering stately university facilities and museums, the home and garden of scientist Carl Linnaeus, as well as a grand cathedral and the enigmatic burial mounds of Gamla Uppsala on the outskirts of town. Note that another side-trip option is to visit a few of the islands in Stockholm's archipelago (described in the next chapter).

Drottningholm Palace

The queen's 17th-century summer castle and current royal residence has been called "Sweden's Versailles." While that's a bit of a stretch, Drottningholm Palace (Drottningholms Slott) is worth ▲▲. It's enjoyable to explore the place where the Swedish royals bunk and to stroll their expansive gardens. Just as worthwhile is touring the nearby **Baroque-era theater** (also rated ▲▲), which preserves 18th-century stage sets and special-effects machinery. You can likely squeeze everything in with half a day here, or linger for an entire day.

GETTING THERE

The castle is an easy boat or subway-plus-bus ride from downtown Stockholm. Consider approaching by water (as the royals tradition-

ally did) and then returning by bus and subway (as a commoner).

Boats depart regularly from near City Hall for the relaxing hour-long trip (145 kr one-way, 195 kr round-trip, discount with Stockholm Card, departs from Stadshus-bron across from City Hall on the hour through the day, likely additional departures at :30 past the hour on weekends or any day in July-Aug, fewer departures Sept-April, tel. 08/1200-4000, www.stromma.se). It can be faster (30-45 minutes total) to take **public transit:** Ride the T-bana about 20 minutes to Brommaplan, where you can catch any #300-series bus for the five-minute ride to Drottningholm (as you leave the Brommaplan Station, check monitors to see which bus is leaving next—usually from platform A, E, or F; 54 kr one-way).

ORIENTATION TO DROTTNINGHOLM PALACE

Cost and Hours: 120 kr, May-Aug daily 10:00-16:30, Sept daily 11:00-15:30, Oct and April Fri-Sun only 11:00-15:30, Nov-March Sat-Sun only 12:00-15:30, closed last two weeks of Dec, tel. 08/402-6280, www.royalcourt.se.

Tours: You can explore the palace on your own, but with sparse posted explanations and no audioguide, it's worth the 20 kr extra for the 30-minute English guided tour, which brings the rooms to life. Tours are offered June-Aug usually at 10:00, 12:00, 14:00, and 16:00 (fewer tours off-season). Alternatively, you could buy the inexpensive palace guidebook.

Services: The gift shop/café at the entrance to the grounds (near the boat dock and bus stop) acts as a visitors center; Drottning-holm's only WCs are in the adjacent building. The café serves light meals. A handy Pressbyrån convenience store is also nearby (snacks, drinks, and transit tickets), and taxis are usually standing by.

BACKGROUND

"Drottningholm" means "Queen's Island." When the original castle mysteriously burned down in 1661 immediately after a visit from Queen

Hedvig Eleonora, she (quite conveniently) had already commissioned plans for a bigger, better palace.

Built over 40 years—with various rooms redecorated by centuries of later monarchs—Drottningholm has the air of overcompensating for an inferiority complex. While rarely absolute rulers, Sweden's royals long struggled with stubborn parliaments. Perhaps this made the propaganda value of the palace decor even more important. Touring the palace, you'll see art that makes the point that Sweden's royalty is divine and belongs with the gods. Portraits and prominently displayed gifts from fellow monarchs attempt to legitimize the royal family by connecting the Swedish blue bloods with Roman emperors, medieval kings, and Europe's great royal families. The portraits you'll see of France's Louis XVI and Russia's Catherine the Great are reminders that Sweden's royalty was related to or tightly networked with the European dynasties.

Of course, today's monarchs are figureheads ruled by a constitution. The royal family makes a point to be as accessible and as "normal" as royalty can be. King Carl XVI Gustaf (b. 1946)—whose main job is handing out Nobel Prizes once a year—is a car nut who talks openly about his dyslexia. He was the first Swedish king not to be crowned "by the grace of God." The popular Queen Silvia is a businessman's daughter. At their 1976 wedding festivities, ABBA serenaded her with "Dancing Queen." Their daughter and heir to the throne, Crown Princess Victoria, studied political science at Yale and interned with Sweden's European Union delegation. In 2010, she married gym owner Daniel Westling—the first royal wedding in Sweden since her parents' marriage. Victoria and Daniel's first child, Princess Estelle, was born on February 23, 2012—and instantly became the next heir to the throne. The king and queen still live in one wing of Drottningholm, while other members of the royal family attempt to live more "normal" lives elsewhere.

VISITING THE PALACE

While not the finest palace interior in Europe (or even in Scandinavia), Drottningholm offers a chance to stroll through a place where a monarch still lives. You'll see two floors of lavish rooms, where Sweden's royalty did their best to live in the style of Europe's divine monarchs.

Ascend the grand staircase (decorated with faux marble and relief-illusion paintings) and buy your ticket on the first floor. Entering the state rooms on the **first floor,** admire the craftsmanship of the walls, with gold leaf shimmering on expertly tooled leather. Then pass through the Green Cabinet and hook right into Hedvig Eleonora's State Bed Chambers. The richly colored Baroque decor here, with gold embellishments, is representative of what the entire interior once looked like. Hedvig Eleonora was a "dowager queen," meaning that she was the widow of a king—her husband, King Karl X, died young at age 24—after they had been married just six years. Looking around the room, you'll see symbolism of this tragic separation. For example, in the ceiling painting, Hedvig Eleonora rides a cloud, with hands joined below her—suggesting that she will be reunited with her beloved in heaven.

This room was also the residence of a later monarch, Gustav III. That's why it looks like (and was) more of a theater than a place for sleeping. In the style of the French monarchs, this is where the ceremonial tucking-in and dressing of the king would take place.

Backtrack into the golden room, then continue down the other hallway. You'll pass through a room of royal portraits with very consistent characteristics: pale skin with red cheeks; a high forehead with gray hair (suggesting wisdom); and big eyes (windows to the soul). At the end of the hall is a grand library, which once held some 7,000 books. The small adjoining room is filled by a large model of a temple in Pompeii; Gustav III—who ordered this built—was fascinated by archaeology, and still today, there's a museum of antiquities named for him at the Royal Palace in Stockholm.

On the **second floor,** as you enter the first room, notice the faux doors, painted on the walls to create symmetry, and the hidden doors for servants (who would scurry—unseen and unheard—through the walls to attend to the royal family). In the Blue Drawing Room is a bust of the then-king's cousin, Catherine the Great. This Russian monarch gave him—in the next room, the Chinese Drawing Room—the (made-in-Russia) faux "Chinese" stove. This dates from a time when exotic imports from China (tea, silk, ivory, Kung Pao chicken) were exciting and new. (Around the same time, in the mid-18th century, the royals built the Chinese Pavilion on Drottningholm's grounds.) The Gobelins tapestries in this room were also a gift, from France's King Louis XVI. In the next room, the darker Oskar Room, are more tapestries—these a gift from England's King Charles I. (Sensing a trend?) You'll pass through Karl XI's Gallery (overlooking the grand staircase)—which is still used for royal functions—and into the largest room on this floor, the Hall of State. The site of royal weddings and receptions, this room boasts life-size paintings of very important Swedes in golden frames and a bombastically painted ceiling.

Drottningholm Palace Park: Like so many European "summer palaces," the Drottningholm grounds are graced with sprawling gardens. Directly behind the palace is the rigid and geometrical Baroque Garden, with angular hedges, tidy rows of trees, fountains, and outdoor "rooms" at the far end. To the right is the English Garden, which has rugged, naturalistic plantings and is speckled with statues. And at the far end of  the grounds, surrounding the Chinese Pavilion, are the Rococo Gardens. While charming, these gardens aren't grand on a European scale—but they are a pretty place for a stroll.

NEAR THE PALACE: DROTTNINGHOLM COURT THEATER

This 18th-century theater (Drottningholms Slottsteater) has miraculously survived the ages—complete with its instruments, hand-operated sound-effects machines for wind, thunder, and clouds; and original stage sets. Visit it on a 40-minute guided tour, which some find more enjoyable than the palace tour.

Cost and Hours: 100 kr for guided tour, English tours about hourly May-Aug 11:00-16:30, Sept 12:00-15:30—these are first and last tour times, shop open before and after, may be limited tours on weekends in April and Oct-Dec, no tours Jan-March, tel. 08/759-0406, www.dtm.se.

Performances: Check their schedule for the rare opportunity to see perfectly authentic operas (about 25 performances each summer). Tickets for this popular time-travel musical and theatrical experience cost 300-1,000 kr and go on sale each March; purchase online (www.ticnet.se), at the theater shop, or by phone (from the US, call +46-77-170-7070; see www.dtm.se for details).

Background: Built by a Swedish king to impress his Prussian wife—who found Sweden dreadfully provincial—this is one of two such historic theaters remaining in Europe (the other is in the town of Český Krumlov, in the Czech Republic). Their son, King Gustav III, loved the theater (some say more than he loved ruling Sweden): Besides ordering Stockholm's Royal Opera to be built, he also wrote, directed, and acted in several theatrical presentations (including the first-ever production in the Swedish language, rather than French). He even died in a theater, assassinated at a masquerade ball in the very opera house he had built. When he died, so too did this flourishing of culture—the theater became a warehouse until it was rediscovered in 1921. Soon thereafter, it began producing plays once again.

Visiting the Theater: On the tour, you'll see the bedrooms where famous actors would sleep while performing here, then enter the theater itself, lit only with (now simulated) candles. You'll see the extremely deep stage (with scenery peeking in from the edges), the royal boxes where the king and queen entered, and doors and curtains that were painted onto walls to achieve perfect symmetry. Be ready to volunteer to try out the old equipment used to make thunder and wind noises. It's fascinating to think that the system of pulleys, trap doors, and actors floating in from the sky isn't so different from the techniques employed on stages today.

Sigtuna

Sigtuna, the oldest town in Sweden (established in the 970s), is the country's cutest town as well. Worth ▲, it sits sugary sweet on Lake Mälaren, about 30 miles inland from Stockholm (reachable by train/bus or sightseeing boat). A visit here affords a relaxed look at an open-air folk museum of a town, with ruined churches, ancient rune stones, and a cobbled lane of 18th-century buildings—all with English info posts. It also offers plenty of shopping and eating options in a park-like lakeside setting. If you're looking for stereotypical Sweden and a break from the big city, Sigtuna is a fun side-trip.

Getting There: By **public transport** from Stockholm, it's a one-hour trip out (take the *pendeltåg* suburban train from Stockholm to Märsta and then change to bus #570). Guided two-hour **sightseeing cruises** run to Sigtuna in summer (350 kr round-trip, Wed-Sun morning departures from Stockholm's Stadshusbron dock, www.stromma.se). If traveling by **car** to Uppsala or Oslo, Sigtuna is a short detour.

Tourist Information: The helpful TI is on the main street and eager to equip you with a town map and info (daily 10:00-18:00, Storagatan 33, tel. 08/5948-0650).

Sights in Sigtuna

Main Street: Storagatan

Sigtuna's main street provides the town's spine. Along it, besides the TI, you'll find the town hall from 1744, with a nicely preserved interior (free, daily 12:00-16:00), and the Sigtuna History Museum, with archaeological finds from the Viking culture here (may be closed for renovation). As you stroll the street, read the historical signs posted along the way and poke into shops and cafés. The most charming place for lunch, a snack, or a drink is Tant Brun ("Auntie Brown's") Café, tucked away just around the corner from the TI in a super-characteristic 17th-century home with a cozy garden.

Churches

Before the Reformation came along, Sigtuna was an important political and religious center, and the site of the country's archbishopric. Along with powerful monastic communities, the town had seven churches. When the Reformation hit, that was the end of the monasteries, and there was a need for only one church—the Gothic Mariakyrkan. It survived, and the rest fell into ruins. Mariakyrkan, or Mary's Church, built by the Dominicans in the 13th century, is decorated with pre-Reformation murals and is worth a look (free, daily 9:00-17:00).

The stony remains of St. Olaf's Church stand in the Mary's Church cemetery. This 12th-century ruin is evocative, with stout vaults and towering walls that served the community as a place of last refuge when under attack.

Rune Stones

Sigtuna is dotted with a dozen rune stones. Literally "word stones," these memorial stones are carved with messages in an Iron Age runic language. Sigtuna has more of these than any other Swedish town. Those here generally have a cross, indicating that they are from the Christian era (11th century). Each is described in English. I like Anund's stone, which says, "Anund had this stone erected in memory of himself in his lifetime." His rune carver showed a glimpse of personality and that perhaps Anund had no friends. (It worked. Now he's in an American guidebook, and 10 centuries later, he's still remembered.)

Uppsala

Uppsala, Sweden's fourth-largest city, is a rather small town with a big history. A few blocks in front of its train station, an inviting commercial center bustles around the main square and along a scenic riverfront. Towering across the river are its historic cathedral and a venerable university. For visitors, the university features a rare 17th-century anatomical theater, an exhibit of its prestigious academic accomplishments, and a library with literary treasures on display. Uppsala is home to the father of modern botany, Carl Linnaeus, whose garden and house—now a museum—make for a fascinating visit. And, just outside town stands Gamla Uppsala, the site of a series of majestic burial mounds where Sweden buried its royalty back in the 6th century. While Gamla Uppsala is a short bus ride away, everything else is within delightful walking distance. If you're not traveling anywhere else in Sweden other than Stockholm, Uppsala (less than an hour away) makes a pleasant day trip. While buzzing during the school year, this university town is sleepy during summer vacations.

GETTING THERE

Take the train from Stockholm's central station (4/hour, 40 minutes, 85 kr; also possible on slower suburban *pendeltåg*—2/hour, 55 minutes, covered by local transit pass plus small supplement). Since the Uppsala station has lockers and is in the same direction from Stockholm as the airport, you could combine a quick visit here with an early arrival or late departure.

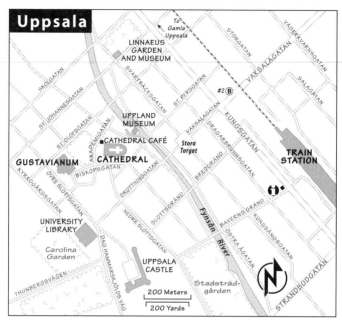

Orientation to Uppsala

TOURIST INFORMATION

The helpful TI, across the street from the train station, has the informative *What's On Uppsala* magazine, which includes the best map of the center and a list of all sights (Mon-Fri 10:00-18:00, Sat 10:00-15:00, Sun July-Aug only 11:00-15:00, Kungsgatan 59, tel. 018/727-4800, www.destinationuppsala.se). They sell the **Uppsala Card** (150 kr, covers all attractions in the city plus bus fare and admission to Gamla Uppsala).

ARRIVAL IN UPPSALA

From the train station (pay lockers), cross the busy street and find the TI on the right (pick up the *What's On* magazine). Walk two blocks to Kungsängsgatan, turn right, and walk to the main square, Stora Torget. The spires of the cathedral mark two of the top three sights (the cathedral itself and the adjacent university buildings). The Linnaeus Garden and Museum is a few blocks up the river, and the bus to Gamla Uppsala is a couple of blocks away (see map, above).

Sights in Uppsala

▲▲UPPSALA CATHEDRAL (UPPSALA DOMKYRKAN)

One of Scandinavia's largest, most historic cathedrals feels as vital as it does impressive. While the building was completed in 1453, the spires and interior decorations are from the late 19th century. The cathedral—with a fine Gothic interior, the relics of St. Erik, memories of countless Swedish coronations, and the tomb of King Gustav Vasa—is well worth a visit.

Cost and Hours: Free, daily 8:00-18:00; guided 45-minute English tours go 1-2 times/day in season (mid-June-mid-Aug Mon-Sat at 11:00 and 14:00, Sun at 15:00), or pick up brochure from gift shop; tel. 018/187-177, www.uppsaladomkyrka.se.

Visiting the Cathedral: Grab a seat in a pew and take in the graceful Gothic lines of the longest nave in Scandinavia (130 yards).

The gorgeously carved, gold-slathered Baroque pulpit is a reminder of the Protestant (post-Reformation) focus on preaching the word of God in the people's language. Look high above in the choir area to enjoy fine murals, restored in the 1970s. For ages, pilgrims have come here to see the relics of St. Erik. All around you are important side chapels, tombs, and memorials (each with an English description).

Near the entrance is the tomb and memorial to scientist Carl Linnaeus, the father of modern botany, who spent his career at the university here (for more on him, see the Linnaeus Garden and Museum listing, later).

In the chapel at the far east end of the church is the tomb of King Gustav Vasa and his family. This chapel was originally dedicated to the Virgin Mary. But Gustav Vasa brought the Reformation to Sweden in 1527 and usurped this prized space for his own tomb. In good Swedish style, the decision was affirmed by a vote in parliament, and bam—the country was Lutheran. (A few years later, England's King Henry VIII tried a similar religious revolution—and had a much tougher time.) Notice that in the tomb sculpture, Gustav is shown flanked by two wives—his first wife died after suffering a fall; his second wife bore him 10 children. High above are murals of Gustav's illustrious life.

Speaking of Mary, notice the modern statue of a common-rather-than-regal Protestant Mary outside the chapel looking in.

This eerily lifelike statue from 2005, called *Mary (The Return)*, captures Jesus' mother wearing a scarf and timeless garb. In keeping with the Protestant spirit here, this new version of Mary is shown not as an exalted queen, but as an everywoman, saddened by the loss of her child and seeking solace—or answers—in the church.

Cathedral Treasury: By the gift shop, you can pay to ride the elevator up to the treasury collection. Here (with the help of a loaner flashlight and English translations), you'll find medieval textiles (tapestries and vestments), swords and crowns found in Gustav's grave, and the Nobel Peace Prize won by Nathan Söderblom, an early-20th-century archbishop here (40 kr, daily 10:00-17:00, until 16:00 in off-season). In this same narthex area, notice the debit-card machine for offerings.

UNIVERSITY ATTRACTIONS AND NEARBY

Scandinavia's first university was founded in Uppsala in 1477. Two famous grads are Carl Linnaeus (the famous botanist) and Anders Celsius (the scientist who developed the temperature scale that bears his name). The campus is scattered around the cathedral part of town, and two university buildings are particularly interesting and welcoming to visitors: the Gustavianum and the library.

▲▲Gustavianum

Facing the cathedral is the university's oldest surviving building, with a bulbous dome that doubles as a sundial (notice the gold numbers). Today it houses a well-presented museum that features an anatomical theater, a cabinet filled with miniature curiosities, and Celsius' thermometer. The collection is curiously engaging for the glimpse it gives into the mindset of 17th-century Europe.

Cost and Hours: 50 kr, June-Aug Tue-Sun 10:00-16:00, Sept-May Tue-Sun 11:00-16:00, closed Mon, Akademigatan 3, tel. 018/471-7571, www.gustavianum.uu.se.

Visiting the Gustavianum: Ride the elevator (near the gift shop/ticket desk) up to the fourth floor. Then, see the exhibits as you walk back down.

Up top is a collection of **Viking artifacts** discovered at Valsgärde, a prehistoric site near Uppsala used for burials for more than 700 years. Archaeologists have uncovered 15 boat graves here (dating from A.D. 600-1050—roughly one per generation), providing insight on the Viking Age. The recovered artifacts on display here show fine Viking workmanship and a society more refined than many might expect.

Next you'll find the **anatomical theater** (accessible from the fourth and third floors). This theater's only show was human dissection. In the mid-1600s, as the enlightened ideas of the Renaissance swept far into the north of Europe, scholars began to consider dissection of the human body the ultimate scientific education. Corpses of hanged criminals were carefully sliced and diced here, under a dome in an almost temple-like atmosphere, demonstrating the lofty heights to which science had risen in society. Imagine 200 students standing tall all around and leaning in to peer intently at the teacher's scalpel. Notice the plaster death masks of the dissected in a case at the entry.

On the second floor is a fascinating exhibit on the **history of the university.** The Physics Chamber features a collection of instruments from the 18th and 19th centuries that were used by university teachers. The Augsburg Art Cabinet takes center stage here with a dizzying array of nearly a thousand miniscule works of art and other tidbits held in an ornately decorated oak cabinet. Built in the 1620s for a bigwig who wanted to impress his friends, the cabinet once held the items shown in display cases all around. Find the interactive video screen, where you can control a virtual tour of the collection. Just beyond the cabinet is a thermometer that once belonged to Celsius (in his handwriting, notice how 0 and 100 were originally flip-flopped, with water boiling at 0 degrees Celsius rather than 100).

On the first floor is the university's **classical antiquities collection** from the Mediterranean. These ancient Greek and Roman artifacts and Egyptian sarcophagi were used to bring classical culture and art to students unable to travel abroad.

▲University Library (Universitetsbiblioteket)
Uppsala University's library, housed in a 19th-century building called the Carolina Rediviva, is a block uphill from the cathedral and Gustavianum. Off the entry hall (to the right) is a small but exquisite exhibit of treasured old books. Well-displayed and well-described in English, the carefully selected collection is surprisingly captivating.

Cost and Hours: Free, daily 9:00-18:00, Dag Hammarskjölds väg 1, tel. 018/471-3941, www.ub.uu.se.

Visiting the Library: With precious items like Mozart scores in the composer's own hand and a map of Mexico City dating from 1555, the display cases here feel like the Treasures room at the British Library.

The most valuable item is the **Silver Bible,** a translation from Greek of the four Gospels into the now-extinct Gothic language. Written in Ravenna in the 6th century, Sweden's single most precious book is so named for its silver-ink writing on purple-colored calfskin vellum. Booty from a 1648 Swedish victory in Prague, it ended up at Uppsala University in 1669.

Another rarity is the **Carta Marina,** the first more-or-less accurate map of Scandinavia, printed in Venice in 1539 from nine woodblocks. Compare this 16th-century understanding of the region with your own travels.

▲Linnaeus Garden and Museum (Linnéträdgården)

Carl Linnaeus, famous for creating the formal system for naming different species of plants and animals, spent his career in Uppsala as a professor. This home, office, greenhouse, and garden is the ultimate Linnaeus sight, providing a vivid look at this amazing scientist and his work.

Cost and Hours: 60 kr for museum and garden; May-Sept Tue-Sun 11:00-17:00, garden open until 20:00, closed Mon and off-season; daily 45-minute English tour at 14:30; after 17:00, when the museum closes, the garden becomes a free public space— enter on Svartbäcksgatan at #27; tel. 018/471-2874, www.linnaeus. uu.se.

Visiting the Garden and Museum: While Linnaeus (whose noble name was Carl von Linné) was professor of medicine and botany at the University of Uppsala, he lived and studied here. From 1743 until 1778, he ran this botanical garden and lived on site to study the plant action—day and night, year-round—of about 3,000 different species. When he moved in, the university's department of medicine and botany moved in as well.

It was in this garden (the first in Sweden, originally set up in 1655) that Linnaeus developed a way to classify the plant kingdom. Wandering the garden where the most famous of all botanists did his work, you can pop into the orangery, built so temperate plants could survive the Nordic winters.

The museum, in Linnaeus' home (which he shared with his wife and seven children), is filled with the family's personal possessions and his professional gear. You'll see his insect cabinet, herbs cabinet, desk, botany tools, and notes. An included audioguide helps bring the exhibit to life.

More Sights near the University

Uppsala has a range of lesser sights, all within walking distance of the cathedral. The **Uppland Museum** (Upplandsmuseet), a regional history museum with prehistoric bits and folk-art scraps, is on the river by the waterfall, near the TI (free, Tue-Sun 12:00-17:00, closed Mon). Uphill from the university library is the 16th-century **Uppsala Castle,** which houses an art museum and runs slice-of-castle-life tours (required 80-kr tour, offered in English only a few weeks each summer Tue-Sun at 13:00 and 15:00, tel. 018/727-2485).

▲GAMLA UPPSALA

This site on the outskirts of town gives historians goose bumps. Gamla Uppsala—literally, "Old Uppsala"—includes nine large royal burial mounds circled by a walking path. Fifteen hundred years ago, when the Baltic Sea was higher and it was easy to sail all the way to Uppsala, the pagan Swedish kings had their capital here. Old Uppsala is where the petty Swedish kingdoms came together and a nation coalesced.

Cost and Hours: The **mounds** are free and always open. The **museum** is 70 kr and open April-Aug daily 11:00-17:00; shorter hours in off-season (generally 12:00-15:00 and closed Tue and Fri); closed in Dec. In summer your museum admission includes a 40-minute guided English tour of the mounds (July-Aug daily at 15:00, tel. 018/239-300, www.raa.se/gamlauppsala). The **church** is free and open daily April-Aug 9:00-18:00, Sept-March 9:00-16:00 (tiny church museum across the lane is free and open Sat-Sun only 12:00-15:00).

Getting There: A direct city bus stops right at the site. From the Uppsala train station, go to the bus stop at Vaksalagatan 7-13 (a block and a half away) and take bus #2, marked *Gamla Uppsala*, to the last stop (30 kr, buy ticket at nearby Pressbyrån kiosk, 2-4/hour, 15-minute trip). All the Gamla Uppsala sights are within 200 yards of each other, making it an easy visit.

Eating: Gamla Uppsala is great for picnics, or you can drop by the rustic and half-timbered Odinsborg café, which serves sandwiches, mead, and daily plates (daily 10:00-18:00, tel. 018/323-525).

Visiting Gamla Uppsala: The highlight of a visit is to climb the evocative mounds, which you're welcome to wander. Also at the site is a small but interesting museum and a 12th-century church.

The Mounds: The focus of ritual and religious activities from the 6th through 13th centuries, the mounds are made meaningful with the help of English info boards posted around.

Imagine the scene over a thousand years ago, when the democratic tradition of this country helped bring the many small Swedish kingdoms together into one nation. A *ting* was a political assembly where people dealt with the issues of the day. Communities would gather here at the rock that marked their place, and then the leader, standing atop the flat mound (nearest today's café), would address the crowd as if in a natural amphitheater. It was here that Sweden became Christianized a thousand years ago. In 1989 Pope John Paul II gave a Mass right here to celebrate the triumph of Christianity over paganism in Sweden. (These days, this is a pretty secular society and relatively few Swedes go to church.)

Museum: Gamla Uppsala's museum gives a good overview of early Swedish history and displays items found in the mounds. While humble, it is instructive, with plenty of excavated artifacts.

Church: Likely standing upon a pagan holy site, the church dates from the 12th century and was the residence of the first Swedish archbishop. An 11th-century rune stone is embedded in the external wall. In the entryway, an iron-clad oak trunk with seven locks on it served as the church treasury back in the 12th century. In the nave, a few Catholic frescoes, whitewashed over in the 16th century with the Reformation, have been restored.

Eating in Uppsala

Survey the many eateries on or near the main square or along the river below the cathedral. The **Cathedral Café** (a few steps to the right as you exit the cathedral) is charming, reasonable, and handy—and your money supports the city's mission of helping the local homeless population (100-kr lunch specials, soup and sandwich menus, Mon-Fri 10:00-17:00, Sat-Sun 11:00-16:00).

STOCKHOLM'S ARCHIPELAGO

Vaxholm • Grinda • Svartsö • Sandhamm

Some of Europe's most scenic islands stretch 80 miles out into the Baltic Sea from Stockholm. If you're cruising to (or from) Finland, you'll get a good look at this island beauty. If you have more time and want to immerse yourself in all that simple Swedish nature, consider spending a day or two island-hopping.

The Swedish word for "island" is simply *ö*, but the local name for this area is Skärgården—literally, "garden of skerries," which are unforested rocks sticking up from the sea. That stone is granite, carved out and deposited by glaciers. The archipelago closer to Stockholm is rockier, with bigger islands and more trees. Farther out (such as at Sandhamn), the glaciers lingered longer, slowly grinding the granite into sand and creating smaller islands.

Locals claim there are more than 30,000 of these islands, and as land here is rising slowly, more pop out every year. Some 150 are inhabited year-round, and about 100 have ferry service. There's an unwritten law of public access in the archipelago: Technically you're allowed to pitch your tent anywhere for up to two nights, provided the owner of the property can't see you from his or her house. It's polite to ask first and essential to act responsibly.

With thousands of islands to choose from, every Swede seems to have a favorite. This chapter covers four very different island destinations that offer an overview of the archipelago. Vaxholm, the gateway to the archipelago, comes with an imposing fortress, a charming fishermen's harbor, and the easiest connections to Stockholm. Rustic Grinda feels like—and used to be—a Swedish summer camp. Sparsely populated Svartsö is another fine back-to-nature experience. And swanky Sandhamn thrills the sailboat set, with a lively yacht harbor, a scenic setting at the far edge of the archipelago, and (true to its name) sandy beaches.

The flat-out best way to experience the magic of the archipelago is simply stretching out comfortably on the rooftop deck  of your ferry. The journey truly is the destination. Enjoy the charm of lovingly painted cottages as you glide by, sitting in the sun on delicate pairs of lounge chairs that are positioned to catch just the right view, with the steady rhythm of the ferries lacing this world together, and people savoring quality time with each other and nature.

PLANNING YOUR TIME

On a Tour: For the best quick look, consider one of the many half- or full-day package boat trips from downtown Stockholm to the archipelago. **Strömma** runs several options, including the three-hour Archipelago Tour (2-4/day, 250 kr), or the all-day Thousand Island Cruise (departs daily in summer at 9:30, 1,150 kr includes lunch and dinner; tel. 08/1200-4000, www.stromma.se).

On Your Own: For more flexibility, freedom, and a better dose of the local vacation scene, do it on your own. Any one of the islands in this chapter is easily doable as a single-day side-trip from Stockholm. And, because all boats to and from Stockholm pass through Vaxholm, it's easy to tack on that town to any other one. For general information about the archipelago, see www.visitskargarden.se.

For a very busy all-day itinerary that takes in the two most enjoyable island destinations (Grinda and Sandhamn), consider this plan: 8:00—Set sail from Stockholm; 9:30—Arrive in Grinda for a quick walk around the island; 10:50—Catch the boat to Sandhamn; 11:45—Arrive in Sandhamn, have lunch, and enjoy the town; 17:00—Catch boat to Stockholm (maybe have dinner on board); 19:05—Arrive back in Stockholm. Or you could craft a route tailored to your interests: For example, for a back-to-nature experience, try Stockholm-Grinda-Svartsö-Stockholm. For an urban mix of towns, consider Stockholm-Vaxholm-Sandhamn-Stockholm.

Overnighting on an island really lets you get away from it all and enjoy the island ambience. I've listed a few island accommodations, but note that midrange options are few; most tend to be either pricey and top-end or very rustic (rented cottages with minimal plumbing).

Don't struggle too hard with the "which island?" decision. The

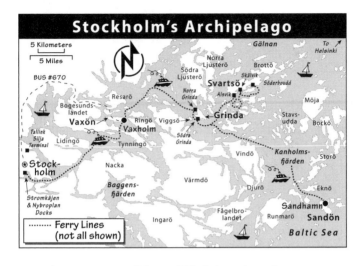

Stockholm's Archipelago

Ferry Lines
(not all shown)

ARCHIPELAGO

main thing is to get well beyond Vaxholm, where the scenery gets more striking. I'd sail an hour or two past Vaxholm, have a short stop on an island, then stop in Vaxholm on the way home. Again, the real joy is the view from your ferry.

GETTING AROUND THE ARCHIPELAGO

A few archipelago destinations (including Vaxholm) are accessible overland, thanks to modern bridges. For other islands, you'll take a boat. Two major companies run public ferries from downtown Stockholm to the archipelago: the bigger Waxholmsbolaget and the smaller Cinderella Båtarna.

Tickets: Regular tickets are sold on board. Simply walk on, and at your convenience, stop by the desk to buy your ticket before you disembark (or wait for them to come around and sell you one). Waxholmsbolaget offers a deal that's worthwhile if you're traveling with a small group or doing a lot of island-hopping. You can save 25 percent by buying a 1,000-kr ticket credit for 750 kr (sold only on land; use the splittable credit to buy tickets on the boat). If you're staying in the archipelago for a few days and want to island-hop, consider the Boat Hopper Pass. This five-day, all-inclusive pass is good on either boat line (420 kr, plus a 20-kr smartcard fee). Buy the card at the Waxholmsbolaget office.

Schedules: Check both companies' schedules when planning your itinerary; you might have to mix and match to make your itinerary work. A single, confusing schedule booklet mixes times for both lines. Ferry schedules are complex even to locals, especially outside of peak season.

Note that the departures mentioned below are for summer (mid-June–mid-Aug); the number of boats declines off-season.

Waxholmsbolaget: Their ships depart from in front of Stockholm's Grand Hotel, at the stop called Stromkäjen (tel. 08/679-5830, www.waxholmsbolaget.se). Waxholmsbolaget boats run from Stockholm to these islands: **Vaxholm** (at least hourly, 1.5 hours, 75 kr), **Grinda** (nearly hourly, 2 hours, 90 kr), **Svartsö** (3/day, 2.5 hours, 110 kr), and **Sandhamn** (1/day, Sat-Sun only, 3.5 hours, 150 kr). These destinations and their timetables are listed in the "Visitor" section of Waxholmsbolaget's website. The same company has routes and schedules throughout the archipelago.

Cinderella Båtarna: This company focuses its coverage on the most popular destinations. Their ships—generally faster, more comfortable, and a little pricier than their rivals'—leave from near Stockholm's Nybroplan, along Strandvägen (tel. 08/1200-4000, www.cinderellabatarna.com). Cinderella boats sail frequently (4/day Mon-Thu, 5/day Fri-Sun) from Stockholm to **Vaxholm** (50 minutes, 110 kr) and **Grinda** (1.5 hours, 145 kr). After Grinda, the line splits, going either to **Sandhamn** (from Stockholm: 1/day Mon-Thu, 2/day Fri-Sun, 2.5 hours, 165 kr), or Finnhamn, with a stop en route at **Svartsö** (from Stockholm: 2/day, 2.5 hours, 165 kr). These fares are for peak season (mid-June–mid-Aug); Cinderella's fares are slightly cheaper off-season.

On Board: When you board, tell the conductor which island you're going to. Boats don't land at all of the smaller islands unless passengers have requested a stop. Hang on to your ticket, as you'll have to show it to disembark. Some boats have luggage-storage areas (ask when you board).

You can usually access the outdoor deck; if you can't get to the front deck (where the boats load and unload), head to the back. Or nab a window seat inside. For the best seat, with less sun and nicer views, I'd go POSH: Port Out, Starboard Home (on the left side leaving Stockholm, on the right side coming back). As you sail, a monitor on board shows the position of your boat as it motors through the islands.

Food: You can usually buy food on board, ranging from simple fare at snack bars to elegant sea-view dinners at fancy restaurants. If your boat has a top-deck restaurant and you want to combine your cruise with dinner, make a reservation as soon as you board. Once you have a table, it's yours for the whole trip, so you can simply claim your seat and enjoy the ride, circling back later to eat. You can also try calling ahead to reserve a table for a specific cruise (for Waxholmsbolaget, call 08/243-090; for Cinderella, call 08/1200-4000).

ARCHIPELAGO

HELPFUL HINTS

Opening Times: Any opening hours I list in this chapter are reliable only for peak season (mid-June–mid-Aug). During the rest of the tourist year ("shoulder season"—late May, early June, late August, and September), hours are flexible and completely weather-dependent; more services tend to be open on weekends than weekdays. Outside the short summer season, many places close down entirely.

Money: Bring cash. The only ATMs are in Vaxholm; farther out, you'll wish you'd stocked up on cash in Stockholm, though most vendors do accept credit cards.

Signal for Stop: At the boat landings or jetties on small islands, you'll notice a small signal tower (called a semaphore) that's used to let a passing boat know you want to be picked up. Pull the cord to spin the white disc and make it visible to the ship. Be sure to put it back before boarding the boat. At night, you signal with light—locals just use their mobile phones.

Weather: The weather on the islands is often better than in Stockholm. For island forecasts, check Götland's (the big island far to the south) instead of Stockholm's.

Local Drink: A popular drink here is *punsch,* a sweet fruit liqueur. Stately old buildings sometimes have *punsch-verandas,* little glassed-in upstairs porches where people traditionally would imbibe and chat.

Vaxholm

The self-proclaimed "gateway to the archipelago," Vaxholm is more developed and less charming than the other islands. Connected by bridge to Stockholm, it's practically a suburb, and not the place to commune with Swedish nature. But it also has an illustrious history as the anchor of Stockholm's naval defense network, and it couldn't be easier to reach (constant buses and boats from Stockholm). While Vaxholm isn't the rustic archipelago you might be looking for, you're almost certain to pass through here at some point on your trip. If you have some extra time, hop off the boat for a visit.

    Getting There: Boats constantly shuttle between Stockholm's waterfront and Vaxholm (1-2/hour, 50 minutes-1.5

hours, 75-110 kr depending on boat company). **Bus #670** runs regularly from the Tekniska Högskolan T-bana stop in northern Stockholm to the center of Vaxholm (3/hour Mon-Fri, 2/hour Sat-Sun, 40-minute trip, 75 kr one-way—three zones). Unless you're on a tight budget, I'd take the boat for the scenery.

Orientation to Vaxholm

Vaxholm, with about 11,000 people, is on the island of Vaxön, connected to the mainland (and Stockholm) by a series of bridges. Everything of interest is within a five-minute walk of the boat dock.

TOURIST INFORMATION

Vaxholm's good TI is well-stocked with brochures about Vaxholm itself, Stockholm, and the archipelago, and can help you with boat schedules (June-Aug Mon-Fri 10:00-18:00, Sat-Sun 10:00-16:00, shorter hours off-season; in the Town Hall building on Rådhustorget, tel. 08/5413-1480, www.vaxholm.se).

ARRIVAL IN VAXHOLM

Ferries stop at Vaxholm's south harbor (Söderhamnen). The **bus** from Stockholm arrives and departs at the bus stop called Söderhamnsplan, a few steps from the boats. To get your bearings, follow my Vaxholm Walk. Luggage lockers are in the Waxholmsbolaget building on the waterfront. The handy electronic departure board (*Nasta Avgang* means "next departure") near the ticket office shows when boats are leaving. For more help, confirm your plans with the person at the ticket office.

Vaxholm Walk

This 30-minute, self-guided, two-part loop will take you to the most characteristic corners of Vaxholm. Begin at the boat dock—you can even start reading as you approach.

Waterfront: Dominating Vaxholm's waterfront is the big Art Nouveau Waxholms Hotell, dating from the early 20th century.

Across the strait to the right is Vaxholm's stout fortress, a reminder of this town's strategic importance over the centuries.

With your back to the water, turn left and walk with the big hotel on your right-hand side. Notice the Waxholmsbolaget office building. Inside you can buy tickets, confirm boat schedules, or stow your bag in a locker. After the hamburger-and-hot-dog stand, you'll reach a roundabout. Just to your left is the stop for bus #670, connecting Vaxholm to Stockholm. Beyond that, a wooden walkway follows the seafront to the town's private boat harbor (Västerhamnen, or "west harbor"), where you can count sailboats and rent a bike.

But for now, continue straight up Vaxholm's appealing, shop-lined main street, Hamngatan. After one long block (notice the handy Coop/Konsum grocery store across the street), turn right up Rådhusgatan (following signs to *Rådhustorget*) to reach the town's main square. The TI is inside the big, yellow Town Hall building on your left. Continue kitty-corner across the square (toward the granite slope) and head downhill on a street leading to the...

Fishermen's Quarter: This Norrhamnen ("north harbor") is ringed by former fishermen's homes. Walk out to the dock and

survey the charming wooden cottages. In the mid-19th century, Stockholmers considered Vaxholm's herring, called *strömming,* top-quality. Caught fresh here, the herring could be rowed into the city in just eight hours and eaten immediately, while herring caught farther out on the archipelago, which had to be preserved in salt, lost its flavor.

As you look out to sea, you'll see a pale green building protruding on the left. This is the charming Hembygdsgården homestead museum, with a pleasant indoor-outdoor café. It's worth heading to this little point (even if the museum is closed, as it often is): As you face the water, go left about one block, then turn right down the gravel lane called Trädgårdsgatan (also marked for *Hembygdsgården*). At this corner, look for the *Strömmingslådan* ("herring shop") sign for the chance to buy what herring connoisseurs consider top-notch fish (summer only).

Continuing down Trädgårdsgatan lane, you'll run right into the **Hembygdsgården homestead.** The big house features an endearing museum showing the simple, traditional fisherman's lifestyle (pop in if it's open; free but donation requested). Next door is a fine café serving sweets and light meals with idyllic outdoor seating (both in front of and behind the museum—look around for your favorite perch, taking the wind direction into consideration). This is the best spot in town for coffee or lunch (see listing under "Sleeping and Eating in Vaxholm," later). From here, look across the inlet at the tiny beach (where we're heading next).

Backtrack to the fishermen's harbor, then continue straight uphill on Fiskaregatan road, and take the first left up the tiny gravel lane marked *Vallgatan.* This part of the walk takes you back

in time, as you wander among old-fashioned wooden homes. At the end of the lane, head left. When you reach the water, go right along a path leading to a thriving little **sandy beach.** In good weather, this offers a fun chance to commune with Swedes at play. (In bad weather, it's hard to imagine anyone swimming or sunning here.)

When you're done relaxing, take the wooden stairs up to the top of the rock and **Battery Park** (Batteripark)—where giant artillery helped Vaxholm flex its defensive muscles in the late 19th century.

As you crest the rock and enjoy the sea views, notice (on your right) the surviving semicircular tracks from those old artillery guns. With a range of 10 kilometers, the recoil from these powerful cannons could shatter glass in nearby houses. Before testing them, they'd play a bugle call to warn locals to stow away their valuables. More artifacts of these defenses are dug into the rock.

To head back to civilization, turn right before the embedded bunker (crossing more gun tracks and passing more fortifications on your left). As you leave the militarized zone, take a left at the fork, and the road will take you down to the embankment—just around the corner from where the boat docks, and our starting point. From along this stretch of embankment, you can catch a boat across the water to Vaxholm Fortress.

Sights in Vaxholm

Vaxholm Fortress and Museum (Vaxholms Kastell/ Vaxholms Fästnings Museum)

Vaxholm's only real attraction is the fortification just across the strait. While the town feels sleepy today, for centuries it was a crucial link in Sweden's nautical defense because it presided over the most convenient passage between Stockholm and the outer archipelago (and, beyond that, the Baltic Sea, Finland, and Russia). The name "Vaxholm" means "Island of

the Signal Fire," emphasizing the burg's strategic importance. In 1548, King Gustav Vasa decided to pin his chances on this loca-

ARCHIPELAGO

tion, ordering the construction of a fortress here and literally filling in other waterways, effectively making this the only way into or out of Stockholm...which it remained for 450 years. A village sprang up across the waterway to supply the fortress, and Vaxholm was born. The town's defenses successfully held off at least two major invasions (Christian IV of Denmark in 1612, and Peter the Great of Russia in 1719). Vaxholm's might gave Sweden's kings the peace of mind they needed to expand their capital to outlying islands— which means that the pint-size powerhouse of Vaxholm is largely to thank for Stockholm's island-hopping cityscape.

Cost and Hours: 60 kr, July-Aug daily 11:15-17:00, June daily 12:15-16:00, first Sat-Sun in Sept 11:15-17:00, closed off-season, tel. 08/5417-1890, www.vaxholmsfastning.se.

Getting There: A ferry shuttles visitors back and forth from Vaxholm (50 kr round-trip, every 20 minutes when museum is open, catch the boat just around the corner and toward the fortress from where the big ferries put in). Once on the island, hike into the castle's inner courtyard and look to the left to find the museum entrance.

Visiting the Fortress: The current, "new" fortress dates from the mid-19th century, when an older castle was torn down and replaced with this imposing granite behemoth. During the 30 years it took to complete the fortress, the tools of warfare changed. Both defensively and offensively, the new fortress was obsolete before it was even completed. The thick walls were no match for the invention of shells (rather than cannonballs), and the high hatches used for attacking tall sailing vessels were useless against new, low-lying, *Monitor*-style attack boats.

Today, the fortress welcomes guests to wander its tough little island and visit its museum. Presented chronologically on two floors (starting upstairs), the modern exhibit traces the military history of this fortress and of Sweden in general. It uses lots of models and mannequins, along with actual weaponry and artifacts, to tell the story right up to the 21st century. There's no English posted, but you can pick up good English translations as you enter. It's as interesting as a museum about Swedish military history can be.

Sleeping and Eating in Vaxholm

Since Vaxholm is so close to Stockholm, there's little reason to sleep here. But in a pinch, Waxholms is the only hotel in town.

Sleeping: **$$$ Waxholms Hotell**'s stately Art Nouveau facade dominates the town's waterfront. Inside are 42 pleasant rooms with classy old-fashioned furnishings (peak-season Sb-1,450 kr, Db-1,750 kr; weekends/July Sb-1,150 kr, Db-1,495 kr; Wi-Fi, loud music some nights in summer—ask what's on and request a

in time, as you wander among old-fashioned wooden homes. At the end of the lane, head left. When you reach the water, go right along a path leading to a thriving little **sandy beach.** In good weather, this offers a fun chance to commune with Swedes at play. (In bad weather, it's hard to imagine anyone swimming or sunning here.)

When you're done relaxing, take the wooden stairs up to the top of the rock and **Battery Park** (Batteripark)—where giant artillery helped Vaxholm flex its defensive muscles in the late 19th century. As you crest the rock and enjoy the sea views, notice (on your right) the surviving semicircular tracks from those old artillery guns. With a range of 10 kilometers, the recoil from these powerful cannons could shatter glass in nearby houses. Before testing them, they'd play a bugle call to warn locals to stow away their valuables. More artifacts of these defenses are dug into the rock.

To head back to civilization, turn right before the embedded bunker (crossing more gun tracks and passing more fortifications on your left). As you leave the militarized zone, take a left at the fork, and the road will take you down to the embankment—just around the corner from where the boat docks, and our starting point. From along this stretch of embankment, you can catch a boat across the water to Vaxholm Fortress.

Sights in Vaxholm

Vaxholm Fortress and Museum (Vaxholms Kastell/ Vaxholms Fästnings Museum)

Vaxholm's only real attraction is the fortification just across the strait. While the town feels sleepy today, for centuries it was a crucial link in Sweden's nautical defense because it presided over the most convenient passage between Stockholm and the outer archipelago (and, beyond that, the Baltic Sea, Finland, and Russia). The name "Vaxholm" means "Island of

the Signal Fire," emphasizing the burg's strategic importance. In 1548, King Gustav Vasa decided to pin his chances on this location, ordering the construction of a fortress here and literally filling in other waterways, effectively making this the only way into or out of Stockholm...which it remained for 450 years. A village sprang up across the waterway to supply the fortress, and Vaxholm was born. The town's defenses successfully held off at least two major invasions (Christian IV of Denmark in 1612, and Peter the Great of Russia in 1719). Vaxholm's might gave Sweden's kings the peace of mind they needed to expand their capital to outlying islands—which means that the pint-size powerhouse of Vaxholm is largely to thank for Stockholm's island-hopping cityscape.

Cost and Hours: 60 kr, July-Aug daily 11:15-17:00, June daily 12:15-16:00, first Sat-Sun in Sept 11:15-17:00, closed off-season, tel. 08/5417-1890, www.vaxholmsfastning.se.

Getting There: A ferry shuttles visitors back and forth from Vaxholm (50 kr round-trip, every 20 minutes when museum is open, catch the boat just around the corner and toward the fortress from where the big ferries put in). Once on the island, hike into the castle's inner courtyard and look to the left to find the museum entrance.

Visiting the Fortress: The current, "new" fortress dates from the mid-19th century, when an older castle was torn down and re-placed with this imposing granite behemoth. During the 30 years it took to complete the fortress, the tools of warfare changed. Both defensively and offensively, the new fortress was obsolete before it was even completed. The thick walls were no match for the in-vention of shells (rather than cannonballs), and the high hatches used for attacking tall sailing vessels were useless against new, low-lying, *Monitor*-style attack boats.

Today, the fortress welcomes guests to wander its tough little island and visit its museum. Presented chronologically on two floors (starting upstairs), the modern exhibit traces the military history of this fortress and of Sweden in general. It uses lots of models and mannequins, along with actual weaponry and artifacts, to tell the story right up to the 21st century. There's no English posted, but you can pick up good English translations as you enter. It's as interesting as a museum about Swedish military history can be.

Sleeping and Eating in Vaxholm

Since Vaxholm is so close to Stockholm, there's little reason to sleep here. But in a pinch, Waxholms is the only hotel in town.

Sleeping: **$$$ Waxholms Hotell**'s stately Art Nouveau fa-cade dominates the town's waterfront. Inside are 42 pleasant rooms with classy old-fashioned furnishings (peak-season Sb-1,450 kr, Db-1,750 kr; weekends/July Sb-1,150 kr, Db-1,495 kr; Wi-Fi, loud music some nights in summer—ask what's on and request a

---

Sleep Code

Abbreviations   (7 kr = about $1, country code: 46, area code: 08)
S = Single, **D** = Double/Twin, **T** = Triple, **Q** = Quad, **b** = bathroom
Price Rankings
   $$$ **Higher Priced**—Most rooms 1,500 kr or more
    $$ **Moderately Priced**—Most rooms 1,000-1,500 kr
     $ **Lower Priced**—Most rooms 1,000 kr or less
Unless otherwise noted, English is spoken, credit cards are accepted, breakfast is included, and Wi-Fi is generally free. Prices change; verify current rates online or by email. For the best prices, always book directly with the hotel.

---

quiet room if necessary, Hamngatan 2, tel. 08/5413-0150, www. waxholmshotell.se, info@waxholmshotell.se). The hotel has a grill restaurant outside in summer and a fancy dining room inside.

Eating: **Hembygdsgården ("Homestead Garden") Café** is Vaxholm's most tempting eatery, serving "summer lunches" (salads and sandwiches) and homemade sweets, with delightful outdoor seating around the Homestead Museum in Vaxholm's characteristic fishermen's quarter. Anette's lingonberry muffins are a treat (light lunches served daily May-Aug, closed Sept-April, tel. 08/5413-1980).

ARCHIPELAGO

Grinda

The rustic, traffic-free isle of Grinda—half retreat, half resort—combines back-to-nature archipelago remoteness with easy proximity to Stockholm. The island is a tasteful gaggle of hotel buildings idyllically situated amid Swedish nature—walking paths, beaches, trees, and slabs of glacier-carved granite sloping into the sea. Since Grinda is a nature preserve (owned by the Stockholm Archipelago Foundation, or Skärgårdsstiftelsen), only a few families actually live here. There's no real town. But in the summer, Grinda becomes a magnet

for day-tripping urbanites, which can make it quite crowded. Adding to its appeal is the nostalgia it holds for many Stockholmers, who fondly recall when this was a summer camp island. In a way, with red-and-white cottages bunny-hopping up its gentle hills and a stately old inn anchoring its center, it retains that vibe today.

Orientation to Grinda

Grinda is small and easy to manage. It's a little wider than a mile in each direction; you can walk from end to end in a half-hour. Its main settlement—the historic **Wärdshus building** (a busy hub of tourist activities), hotel, and related amenities—sits next to its harbor, where private yachts and sailboats put in. Everything on the island is owned and operated by the same company; fortunately, it does a tasteful job of managing the place to keep the island's relaxing personality intact.

Major points of interest are well-signposted in Swedish: *Södra Bryggan* (south dock), *Norra Bryggan* (north dock), *Värdshus* (hotel at the heart of the island), *Gästhamn* (guest harbor); *Affär* (general store); *stuga/stugby* (cottage/s); *Grindastigen* (nature trail); and *Tältplats* (campground).

TOURIST INFORMATION

The red cottage marked *Expedition* greets arriving visitors just up the hill from the Södra Grinda ferry dock. The staff answers questions, and the cottage serves as a small shop, a place to rent kayaks or saunas, and a reception desk for the island's cottages and hostel (open daily in season; general info tel. 08/5424-9491, www.archipelagofoundation.se).

ARRIVAL IN GRINDA

Public ferries use one of two docks, at opposite ends of the island: Most use Södra Grinda to the south (nearest the hostel and cottages), while a few use Norra Grinda to the north (closer to the campground). From either of these, it's about a 10- to 15-minute walk to the action.

Sights in Grinda

Grinda is made to order for strolling through the woods, taking a dip, picnicking, and communing with Swedish nature. Watch the

boats bob in the harbor and work on your Baltic tan. You can simply stick to the gravel trails connecting the island's buildings, or for more nature, take the Grindastigen trail, which loops to the far end of the island and back in less than an hour (signposted from near the Wärdshus).

You can also rent a kayak or rent the private little sauna hut bobbing in the harbor. There's no bike rental here—and the island is a bit too small to keep a serious biker busy—but you could bring one on the boat from Stockholm.

As you stroll, you might spot a few haggard-looking tents through the trees. The right to pitch a tent here was established by the Swedish government during World War II, to give the downtrodden a cheap place to sleep. Those permissions are still valid, inherited, bought, and sold, which means that Grinda has a thriving community of tent-dwelling locals who camp out here all summer long (April-Oct). While some may be the descendants of those original hobos, these days they choose this lifestyle and live as strange little barnacles attached to Grinda. Once each summer they have a progressive tent-crawl bender before heading to the Wärdshus to blow a week's food budget on a fancy meal.

The island just across from the Södra Grinda dock (to the right) is Viggsö, where the members of ABBA have summer cottages and wrote many of their biggest hits.

Sleeping in Grinda

You have various options, in increasing order of rustic charm: hotel, hostel, and cottages. You can reserve any of these through the Grinda Wärdshus. This hub of operations has a restaurant, bar, Wi-Fi, and conference facilities (tel. 08/5424-9491, www.grinda. se, info@grinda.se).

Grinda is busiest in the summer, when tourists fill its hotel; in spring and fall, it mostly hosts conferences. If sleeping at the hostel or cottages, arrange arrival details (you'll probably pick up your keys at the *Expedition* shed near the dock). The hostel and cottages charge extra for bed linens. If you have a tent, you can pitch it at the basic campsite near the north jetty for a small fee.

ARCHIPELAGO

$$$ Grinda Hotel rents 30 rooms (each named for a local bird or fish) in four buildings just above the Wärdshus. These are modern, comfortable, and made for relaxing, intentionally lacking distractions such as TVs or phones (Sb-1,600 kr, Db-2,000 kr, larger suite-2,600 kr, 120 kr less/person if you skip breakfast, extra bed-400 kr, if dining at the restaurant the "Wärdshus package" will save you a few kronor).

$ The 27 **cottages**—most near the Södra Grinda ferry dock—are rentable, offering a rustic retreat (kitchenettes but no running water, shared bathroom facilities outside). From mid-June to mid-August, these come with a one-week minimum and cost more (2-bed cottage-3,000 kr/week, 4-bed cottage-3,500 kr/week, 6-bed cottage-4,000 kr; at other times rentable by the night: 2-bed-1,000 kr, 4-bed-1,200 kr, 6-bed-1,500 kr).

$ Grinda Hostel (Vandrarheim) is the place to sleep if you wish you'd gone to Swedish summer camp as a kid. The 44 bunks are in simple two- and four-bed cottages, surrounding a pair of fire pits (300 kr/bed regardless of room size, great shared kitchen/dining hall). A small pebbly beach and a basic sauna are nearby.

Eating in Grinda

All your options (aside from bringing your own picnic from Stockholm) are run by the hotel, with choices in each price range.

Grinda Wärdshus, the inn at the center of the complex, has a good restaurant that combines rural island charm with fine food. You can choose between traditional Swedish meals and contemporary international dishes. Servings are small but thoughtfully designed to be delicious. Eat in the woody dining room or on the terrace out front (1,395 kr/person covers dinner and double room, 140-170-kr starters, 190-300-kr main dishes; open late June-Aug daily 12:00-24:00; weekends only—and some Fri—in off-season).

Grindas Framfickan ("Grinda's Front Pocket") is a pleasant bistro that serves up basic but tasty food (such as fish burgers and grilled shrimp) right along the guest harbor. Order at the counter, then choose a table to wait for your food (140-200-kr dishes, early June-mid-Aug daily 11:00-22:00, otherwise sporadically open in good weather—especially weekends).

The **general store and café** (Lanthandel) just below the Wärdshus is the place to rustle up some picnic fixings. You'll also find coffee to go, ice cream, "one-time grills" for a disposable barbecue, and kayak rentals (open long hours daily early June-mid-Aug, Fri-Sun only in shoulder season).

Svartsö

The remote and lesser-known isle of Svartsö (svert-show, literally "Black Island"), a short hop beyond Grinda, is the "Back Door" option of the bunch. Unlike Grinda, Svartsö is home to a real community; islanders have their own school and library. But with only 80 year-round residents, the old generation had to specialize. Each person learned a skill to fill a niche in the community—one guy was a carpenter, the next was a plumber, the next was an electrician, and so on. While the island is less trampled than the others in this chapter (just one B&B and a great restaurant), it is reasonably well-served by ferries. Svartsö feels remote and potentially even boring for those who aren't wowed by simply strolling through meadows. But it's ideal for those who want to slow down and immerse themselves in nature.

Svartsö hosts the school for this part of the archipelago. Because Swedish law guarantees the right to education, even kids living on remote islands are transported to class. A school boat trundles from island to island each morning to collect kids headed for the school on Svartsö. If the weather is bad, a hovercraft retrieves them. If it's really bad, and all of the snow days have been used up, a helicopter takes the kids to school.

Orientation to Svartsö: The island, about five miles long and a half-mile wide, has three docks. The main one, at the southwestern tip, is called Alsvik (with the general store and restaurant). Halfway up is Skälvik (near the B&B), and at the northeastern end is Söderboudd. Most boats stop at Alsvik, but if you want to go to a different dock, you can request a stop (ask the conductor on board, or use the semaphore signal at the dock).

At the **Alsvik dock,** the great little general store, called Svartsö Lanthandel, sells anything you could need and also acts as the town TI, post office, and liquor store (open daily mid-May-mid-Aug, more sporadic in off-season but open year-round, tel. 08/5424-7325). You can rent bikes here; in busy times, call ahead to reserve one. The little café on the dock sells drinks and light food, and rents cottages (shared outdoor toilets, tel. 08/5424-7110).

The island has a few paved lanes and almost no traffic. Residents own three-wheeled utility motorbikes for hauling things to and from the ferry landing. The interior consists of little more than trees. With an hour or so, you can bike across the island and back, enjoying the mellow landscape and chatting with the friendly big-city people who've found their perfect escape.

Eating in Svartsö: If you leave the Alsvik dock to the right and walk five minutes up the hill, you'll find the excellent **Svartsö Krog** restaurant. Opened by a pair of can-do foodies who also run a top-end butcher shop at a Stockholm market hall, this place has a deep respect for the sanctity of meat. Specializing in well-constructed, ingredient-driven dishes, the restaurant brings Stockholm culinary sophistication to a castaway island. Choose one of the three eating zones (each with the same menu): outside, the upscale dining room, or in the original pub interior (an Old West-feeling tavern that the new owner has kept as-is to respect the old-timers). The menu is pricey but good (100-200-kr starters, 175-300-kr main dishes). Their specialty is "golden entrecôte," grilled steak that's been aged for eight weeks (open for lunch and dinner daily June-Aug; May and Sept open Thu-Sun for dinner, as well as lunch on Sat-Sun; closed Oct-April; tel. 08/5424-7255).

Sandhamn

Out on the distant fringe of the archipelago—the last stop before Finland—sits the proud village of Sandhamn (on the island of Sandön). Literally "Sand Harbor," this is where the glacier got hung up and kept on churning away, grinding stone into sand. The town has a long history as an important and posh place. In 1897, the Royal Swedish Sailing Society built its clubhouse here, putting Sandhamn on the map as the yachting center of the Baltic—  Sweden's answer to Nantucket. It remains an extremely popular stop for boaters—from wealthy yachties to sailboat racers—as well as visitors simply seeking a break from the big city.

The island of Sandön feels stranded on the edge of the archipelago, rather than immersed in it. Sandhamn is on its sheltered side. Though it's far from Stockholm, Sandhamn is very popular. During the peak of summer (mid-June through late August), it's extremely crowded. Expect to stand in line, and call ahead for restaurant reservations. But even during these times, the Old Town is relatively peaceful and pleasant to explore. If the weather's decent, shoulder season is delightful (though it can be busy on weekends).

Orientation to Sandhamn

You'll find two halves to Sandhamn: In the shadow of that still-standing iconic yacht clubhouse is a ritzy resort/party zone throbbing with big-money nautical types. But just a few steps away, around the harbor, is an idyllic time-warp Old Town of colorfully painted

shiplap cottages tucked between tranquil pine groves. While most tourists come here for the resort, the quieter part of Sandhamn holds the real appeal.

Sandhamn has a summer-only **TI** (open June-mid-Aug) in the harbor area (www.destinationsandhamn.se.)

Sandhamn Walk

To get your bearings from the ferry dock, take this self-guided walk. Begin by facing out to sea.

As you look out to the little point across from the dock, notice the big yellow building. In the 18th century, this was built as the

pilot house. Because the archipelago is so treacherous to navigate—with its tens of thousands of islands and skerries, not to mention untold numbers of hidden underwater rocks—locals don't trust outsiders to bring their boats here. So passing ships unfamiliar with these waters were required to pick up a local captain (or "pilot") to take them safely all the way to Stockholm. The tradition continues today. The orange boats marked *pilot*, moored below the house, ferry loaner captains to oncoming ships. And, since this is the point of entry into Sweden, foreign ships can also be processed by customs here.

The little red shed just in front of the pilot house is home to a humble **town museum** that's open sporadically in the summer, featuring exhibits on Sandhamn's history and some seafaring tales. Just below that, notice the waterfront red barn with the *T* sign. The owner of this boat-repair shop erected this marker for Stockholm's T-bana just for fun.

Just above the barn, look for the yellow building with the blue letters spelling **Sandhamns Värdshus.** This traditional inn, built in the late 17th century, housed sailors while they waited here to set out to sea. During that time, Stockholm had few exports, so ships that brought and unloaded cargo there came to Sandhamn to load up their holds with its abundant sand as ballast. Today the inn still serves good food (see "Eating in Sandhamn," later).

Stretching to the left of the inn are the quaint storefronts of most of Sandhamn's **eateries** (those that aren't affiliated with the big hotel)—bakery, deli, and grocery store, all of them humble but just right for a simple bite or picnic shopping. Local merchants enjoy a pleasantly symbiotic relationship. Rather than try to compete with each other, they attempt to complement what the next shop sells—each one finding just the right niche.

The area stretching beyond these storefronts is Sandhamn's **Old Town**—a maze of wooden cottages that's an absolute delight to explore (and easily the best activity in town). Only 50 of Sandhamn's homes (of around 450) are occupied by year-rounders. The rest are summer cottages of wealthy Stockholmers, or bunkhouses for seasonal workers in the tourist industry. Most locals live at the farthest-flung (and therefore least desirable) locations. Imagine the impact of 100,000 annual visitors on this little town.

Where the jetty meets the island, notice (on the right) the old-fashioned telephone box with the fancy *Rikstelefon* logo. It con-

tains the island's lone working pay phone. Just to the right of the phone box, you can see the back of the town's bulletin board, where locals post their classified ads. To the left at the base of the dock is Sandhamns Kiosk, a newsstand selling local and international publications (as well as candy and ice cream). A bit farther to the left, the giant red building with the turret on top is the **yacht clubhouse** that put Sandhamn on the map, and still entertains the upper crust today with a hotel, several restaurants, spa, mini-golf course, outdoor pool, and more. You'll see its proud SSS-plus-crown logo (standing for Svenska Segelsällskapet—Swedish Sailing Society) all over town. In the 1970s, the building was owned by a notorious mobster who made meth in the basement, then smuggled it out beneath the dock to sailboats moored in the harbor.

Spinning a bit farther to the left, back to where you started, survey the island across the strait (Lökholmen). Just above the trees, notice the copper dome of an observatory that was built by this island's eccentric German oil-magnate owner in the early 20th

ARCHIPELAGO

century. He also built a small castle (not quite visible from here) for his kids to play in.

For a narrated stroll to another fine viewpoint, walk into town and turn left along the water. After about 50 yards, a sign on the right points up a narrow lane to *Post*. This unassuming gravel path is actually one of Sandhamn's most important streets, with the post office, police department (which handles only paperwork—real crimes are deferred to the Stockholm PD), and doctor (who visits town every second Wednesday). While Sandhamn feels remote, it's served—like other archipelago communities—by a crack emergency-response network that can dispatch a medical boat or, in extreme cases, a helicopter. With top-notch hospitals in Stockholm just a 10-minute chopper ride away, locals figure that if you have an emergency here, you might just make it to the doctor faster than if you're trying to make it through congested city streets in an ambulance. At the end of this lane, notice the giant hill of the town's namesake sand.

Continuing along the main tree-lined harborfront strip, you can't miss the signs directing yachters to the *toalett* (toilet) and *sopor* (garbage dump). Then you'll pass the Sandhamns Guiderna office, a **travel agency** where you can rent bikes, kayaks, and fishing gear (tel. 08/640-8040). Just after that is the barn for the volunteer fire department (Brandstation). With all the wooden buildings in town, fire is a concern—one reason why Sandhamn restricts camping (and campfires).

Go beneath the skyway connecting the big red hotel to its modern annex. Then veer uphill (right) at the *Badstranden Trouville* sign, looking down at the mini-golf course. After you crest the top of the hill, on the left is a big, flat expanse of rock nicknamed Dansberget ("Dancing Rock") because it once hosted community dances with a live orchestra. Walk out to enjoy fine **views** of the Baltic

Sea—from here, boaters can set sail for Finland, Estonia, and St. Petersburg, Russia. Looking out to the horizon, notice the three lighthouse towers poking up from the sea, used to guide ships to this gateway to the archipelago. The finish line for big boat races stretches across this gap (from the little house on the point to your left). In summer, this already busy town gets even more jammed with visitors, thanks to the frequent sailing races that end here. The

ARCHIPELAGO

biggest annual competition is the Götlandrunt, a round-trip from here to the island of Götland. In 2009, Sandhamn was proud to be one of just 10 checkpoints on the Volvo Ocean Race, a nine-month race around the world that called mostly at bigger cities (such as Boston, Singapore, and Rio).

Our walk is finished. You can head back into town. Or, to hit the beach, continue another 15 minutes to Trouville beach (explained below).

Sights in Sandhamn

Beaches (Stränder)

True to its name, Sandön ("Sandy Island") has some of the archipelago's rare sandy beaches. The closest, and local favorite, is the no-name beach tucked in a cove just behind the Old Town (walk through the community from the main boat dock, then follow the cove around to the little sandy stretch).

The most popular—which can be quite crowded in summer—is Trouville beach, at the opposite end of the island from Sandhamn (about a 20-minute walk). To find it, walk behind the big red hotel and take the right, uphill fork (marked with the low-profile *Badstranden Trouville* sign) to the "Dancing Rock," then proceed along the road. Take a left at the fork by the tennis courts, then walk about 10 minutes through a mysterious-feeling forest until you reach a little settlement of red cottages. Take a right at the fork (look up for the *Till Stranden* sign), and then, soon after, follow the middle fork (along the plank walks) right to the beach zone: two swathes of sand marked off by rocks, stretching toward Finland.

Sleeping in Sandhamn

Sandhamn has a pair of very expensive top-end hotels, a basic but comfortable B&B, and little else. If you're sleeping on Sandhamn, the B&B is the best choice.

$$$ Sands Hotell is a stylish splurge sitting proudly at the top of town. While oriented mostly to conferences and private parties, its 19 luxurious rooms also welcome commoners in the summer (Sb-2,100 kr, Db-2,500 kr, Wi-Fi, elevator, spa, tel. 08/5715-3020, www.sandshotell.se, info@sandshotell.se).

$$$ Sandhamns Seglarhotellet rents 79 nautical-themed rooms in a modern annex behind the old yacht club building (where you'll find the reception). The rooms are fine, but the prices are sky-high (Db-2,390 kr, 200 kr more for balcony, extra bed-400 kr, small apartment-2,590 kr, large apartment-2,890 kr, suite-4,090 kr, Wi-Fi, loud music from disco inside the clubhouse—light sleepers should ask for a quieter back room, great gym and pool area, tel. 08/5745-0400, www.sandhamn.com, reception@sandhamn.com).

$ Sandhamns Värdshus B&B rents five rustic but tasteful, classically Swedish rooms in an old mission house buried deep in the colorful Old Town. To melt into Sandhamn and get away from the yachties, sleep here (S-930 kr, D-1,350 kr, mostly twins, all rooms share WC and shower, tiny cottage with its own bathroom for same price, includes breakfast, reception is at the restaurant—see below, tel. 08/5715-3051, www.sandhamns-vardshus.se, info@sandhamns-vardshus.se). The rooms are above a reception hall that is rented out for events, but after 22:00, quiet time kicks in.

Eating in Sandhamn

IN THE OLD TOWN

Sandhamn's most appealing eateries are along the Old Town side of the harbor.

Sandhamns Värdshus, right on the water, is the town's best eatery. They serve traditional Swedish food in three separate dining zones (which mostly share the same menu, but each also has its own specials): out on an inviting deck overlooking the water; upstairs in a salty dining room with views; or downstairs in a simple pub (open daily for lunch and dinner nearly year-round, tel. 08/5715-3051).

To grab a bite or assemble a picnic, browse through these smaller eateries (listed in the order you'll reach them from the boat dock): **Westerbergs Livsmedel** grocery store has basic supplies (open sporadic hours daily). **Dykarbaren Café** serves lunches and dinners with indoor and outdoor seating (open daily mid-June-mid-Aug, Wed-Sun only in shoulder season, closed off-season; tel. 08/5715-3554). **Monrads Deli** is a bright, innovative shop where you can buy sandwiches and salads, a wide array of meats for grilling, cheeses, cold cuts, drinks, fresh produce, and other high-quality picnic fixings (open long hours daily in summer, mobile 0709-650-300). Just around the corner (uphill from the harbor and behind the

Värdsgasthus), **Sandhamns Bageriet,** a popular bakery/café serving coffee, sweet rolls, and sandwiches, is a great early-morning venue (daily in summer).

AMONG THE YACHTIES

Sandhamn Seglarhotell has several eateries, open to guests and non-guests. Out on the dock is the Seglargrillen, an American-style grill with a takeout window and outdoor tables (85-kr dishes, open in summer in good weather only). Upstairs in the building's main ballroom is an eatery serving good but pricey Swedish and international food (150-200-kr starters, 185-300-kr main courses, traditional daily lunch special for 145 kr). The restaurant enjoys fine sea views and has a bar/dance hall zone (with loud disco music until late, nearly nightly in summer). Down on the ground floor is a pub/nightclub (tel. 08/5745-0421).

ARCHIPELAGO

PRACTICALITIES

This section covers just the basics on traveling in this region (for much more information, see *Rick Steves Scandinavia*). You'll find free advice on specific topics at www.ricksteves.com/tips.

Money

Sweden uses the Swedish kroner: 1 krona equals about $0.15. To roughly convert prices in kroner to dollars, divide prices by 7 (100 kr = about $14). Check www.oanda.com for the latest exchange rates.

The standard way for travelers to get kroner is to withdraw money from ATMs using a debit or credit card, ideally with a Visa or MasterCard logo. Before departing, call your bank or credit-card company: Confirm that your card(s) will work overseas, ask about international transaction fees, and alert them that you'll be making withdrawals in Europe. Also ask for the PIN number for your credit card in case it'll help you use Europe's "chip-and-PIN" payment machines (see below); allow time for your bank to mail your PIN to you. To keep your valuables safe while traveling, wear a money belt.

Dealing with "Chip and PIN": Much of Europe (including Sweden) is adopting a "chip-and-PIN" system for credit cards, and some merchants rely on it exclusively. European chip-and-PIN cards are embedded with an electronic chip, in addition to the magnetic stripe used on our American-style cards. This means that your credit (and debit) card might not work at payment machines, such as those at train and subway stations, toll roads, parking garages, luggage lockers, and self-serve gas pumps. Memorizing your credit card's PIN lets you use it at some chip-and-PIN machines—just enter the PIN when the machine asks for the "kod." If a machine won't take your card, look for a machine that takes cash or see if there's a cashier nearby who can process your transaction. Often the easiest solution is to pay for your purchases with cash you've withdrawn from an ATM using your debit card (Europe's ATMs still accept magnetic-stripe cards).

Phoning

Smart travelers use the telephone to reserve or reconfirm rooms, reserve restaurants, get directions, research transportation connections, confirm tour times, phone home, and lots more.

To call Sweden from the US or Canada: Dial 011-46 and then the area code (minus its initial zero) and local number. (The 011 is our international access code, and 46 is Sweden's country code.)

To call Sweden from a European country: Dial 00-46 followed the area code (minus its initial zero) and local number. (The 00 is Europe's international access code.)

To call within Sweden: If you're dialing within an area code, just dial the local number; but if you're calling outside your area code, you have to dial both the area code (which starts with a 0) and the local number.

Tips on Phoning: A mobile phone—whether an American one that works in Sweden, or a European one you buy when you arrive—is handy, but can be pricey. If traveling with a smartphone, consider getting an international plan from your provider and try to switch off data-roaming until you have free Wi-Fi. With Wi-Fi, you can use your smartphone to make free or inexpensive domestic and international calls by taking advantage of a calling app such as Skype, FaceTime, or Google+ Hangouts.

To make cheap international calls, you can buy an international phone card in Sweden; these work with a scratch-to-reveal PIN code at any phone, allow you to call home to the US for pennies a minute, and also work for domestic calls.

Another option is buying an insertable phone card in Sweden. These are usable only at pay phones, are reasonable for making calls within the country, and work for international calls as well (though not as cheaply as the international phone cards). However, pay phones are becoming hard to find in Scandinavian countries. You're likely to see them only in railway stations, airports, and medical facilities. Note that insertable phone cards—and most international phone cards—work only in the country where you buy them.

Calling from your hotel-room phone is usually expensive, unless you use an international phone card. For more on phoning, see www.ricksteves.com/phoning.

From:	rick@ricksteves.com
Sent:	Today
To:	info@hotelcentral.com
Subject:	Reservation request for 19-22 July

Dear Hotel Central,

I would like to reserve a room for 2 people for 3 nights, arriving 19 July and departing 22 July. If possible, I would like a quiet room with a double bed and a bathroom inside the room.

Please let me know if you have a room available and the price.

Thank you!
Rick Steves

Making Hotel Reservations

To ensure the best value, I recommend reserving rooms in advance, particularly during peak season. Email the hotelier with the following key pieces of information: number and type of rooms; number of nights; date of arrival; date of departure; and any special requests. (For a sample form, see the sidebar.) Use the European style for writing dates: day/month/year. Hoteliers typically ask for your credit-card number as a deposit.

Some hotels are willing to deal to attract guests—try emailing several to ask their best price. Most Scandinavian business hotels use "dynamic pricing," which means they change the room rate depending on demand—just like the airlines change their fares. This makes it extremely difficult to predict what you will pay. For many hotels, I list a range of prices. If the rate you're offered is at or near the bottom of my printed range, it's likely a good deal.

In general, hotel prices can soften if you do any of the following: offer to pay cash, stay at least three nights, or mention this book. You can also try asking for a cheaper room or a discount, or offer to skip breakfast. Even though most hotels in Sweden base their prices on demand, it is possible to find lower prices during the summer and on weekends. Check hotel websites for deals.

Eating

Restaurants are often expensive. Alternate between picnics (outside or in your hotel or hostel); cheap, forgettable, but filling cafeteria or fast-food fare ($20 per person); and atmospheric, carefully chosen restaurants popular with locals ($40 per person and up). Ethnic eateries—Turkish, Greek, Italian, and Asian—offer a good value and a break from Swedish food.

If you want to enjoy a combination of picnics and restaurant meals on your trip, you'll save money by eating in restaurants at lunch (when there's usually a daily special—*dagens rätt*—and food is generally cheaper), then picnicking for dinner.

The *smörgåsbord* is a revered Scandinavian culinary tradition. Seek it out at least once during your visit. Begin with the fish dishes, along with boiled potatoes and *knäckebröd* (Swedish crisp bread). Then move on to salads, egg dishes, and various cold cuts. Next it's meatball time! Pour on some gravy as well as a spoonful of lingonberry sauce. Still hungry? Make a point to sample the Nordic cheeses and the racks of traditional desserts, cakes, and custards.

Hotel breakfasts are a huge and filling buffet, generally included but occasionally a $12-or-so option. It usually features fruit, cereal, various milks, breads, crackers, cold cuts, pickled herring, caviar paste, and boiled eggs.

In Sweden, most alcohol is sold only at state-run liquor stores called Systembolaget (though weak beer is available at supermarkets). To avoid extremely high restaurant prices for alcohol, many Swedes—and tourists—buy their wine, beer, or spirits at a store and then drink at a public square; this is illegal although often done. One local specialty is *akvavit*, a strong, vodka-like spirit distilled from potatoes and flavored with anise, caraway, or other herbs and spices—then drunk ice-cold. *Lakka* is a syrupy-sweet liqueur made from cloudberries, the small orange berries grown in the Arctic.

Service: Good service is relaxed (slow to an American). When you want the bill, say, *"Kan jag få notan, tack."* Throughout Sweden, a service charge is included in your bill, so there's no need to leave an additional tip. In fancier restaurants or any restaurant where you enjoy great service, round up the bill (about 5-10 percent of the total check).

Transportation

By Train and Bus: Trains cover many Scandinavian destinations. If you're traveling beyond Stockholm and want to see if a railpass could save you money, check www.ricksteves.com/rail. If you're buying tickets as you go, note that prices can fluctuate. To research train schedules and fares, visit the Swedish train website: www.sj.se. Nearly any long-distance train ride requires you to make a reservation before boarding (the day before is usually fine).

Don't overlook long-distance buses (e.g., between Stockholm and Oslo), which are usually slower than trains but have considerably cheaper and more predictable fares. Sweden's biggest bus carrier is Swebus (www.swebusexpress.se).

By Car: It's cheaper to arrange most car rentals from the US. For tips on your insurance options, see www.ricksteves.com/cdw, and for route planning, consult www.viamichelin.com. Bring your driver's license. Local road etiquette is similar to that in the US. Ask your car-rental company about the rules of the road, or check the US State Department website (www.travel.state.gov, click on "International Travel," then specify your country of choice and click "Traffic Safety and Road Conditions"). Use your headlights day and night; it's required in most of Scandinavia. A car is a worthless headache in Stockholm—there's a congestion tax to enter the city center on weekdays. If you must drive into the city, park it safely (get tips from your hotelier).

By Boat: Boats are romantic, scenic, and sometimes the most efficient—or only—way to link destinations in coastal Sweden. Note that short-distance ferries may take only cash, not credit cards. Advance reservations are recommended when using overnight boats in summer or on weekends to link Stockholm with Helsinki (www.vikingline.fi and www.tallinksilja.com). For cruising the nearby islands, see the Stockholm's Archipelago chapter.

By Plane: SAS is the region's dominant airline (www.flysas.com) and operates a low-cost Finnish subsidiary called Blue1 (hubs in Helsinki and Stockholm, www.blue1.com). Well-known cheapo airlines easyJet (www.easyjet.com) and Ryanair (www.ryanair.com) fly into Scandinavia.

Helpful Hints

Emergency Help: To summon the **police** or an **ambulance**, dial 112. For passport problems, call the **US Embassy** (in Stockholm: passport services by appointment only, info tel. 08/783-4375—available Mon-Tue and Thu 13:00-14:00, emergency tel. 08/783-5300, http://stockholm.usembassy.gov).

If you have a minor illness, do as the locals do and go to a pharmacist for advice. Or ask at your hotel for help—they'll know of the nearest medical and emergency services. For other concerns, get advice from your hotelier.

Theft or Loss: To replace a passport, you'll need to go in person to an embassy (see above). Cancel and replace your credit and debit cards by calling these 24-hour US numbers collect: Visa—tel. 303/967-1096, MasterCard—tel. 636/722-7111, American Express—tel. 336/393-1111. In Sweden, to make a collect call to the US, dial 020-799-111; press zero or stay on the line for an operator. File a police report either on the spot or within a day or two; you'll need it to submit an insurance claim for lost or stolen railpasses or electronics, and it can help with replacing your passport or credit and debit cards. Precautionary measures can minimize the effects of loss—back up your photos and other files frequently. For more information, see www.ricksteves.com/help.

Time: Europe uses the 24-hour clock. It's the same through

12:00 noon, then keep going: 13:00, 14:00, and so on. Sweden, like most of continental Europe, is six/nine hours ahead of the East/West Coasts of the US.

Holidays and Festivals: Europe celebrates many holidays, which can close sights and attract crowds (book hotel rooms ahead). For more on holidays and festivals in Sweden, check the Scandinavia Tourist Board website: www.goscandinavia.com. For a simple list showing major—though not all—events, see www.ricksteves.com/festivals.

Numbers and Stumblers: What Americans call the second floor of a building is the first floor in Europe. Europeans write dates as day/month/year, so Christmas 2016 is 25/12/16. Commas are decimal points and vice versa—a dollar and a half is 1,50, and there are 5.280 feet in a mile. Europe uses the metric system: A kilogram is 2.2 pounds; a liter is about a quart; and a kilometer is six-tenths of a mile.

Resources from Rick Steves

This Snapshot guide is excerpted from the latest edition of *Rick Steves Scandinavia,* which is one of more than 30 titles in my series of guidebooks on European travel. I also produce a public television series, *Rick Steves' Europe,* and a public radio show, *Travel with Rick Steves.* My website, www.ricksteves.com, offers free travel information, a forum for travelers' comments, guidebook updates, my travel blog, an online travel store, and information on European railpasses and our tours of Europe. If you're bringing a mobile device on your trip, you can download my Rick Steves Audio Europe app, featuring podcasts of my radio shows, free audio tours of major sights in Europe, and travel interviews about Sweden. You can get Rick Steves Audio Europe via Apple's App Store, Google Play, or the Amazon Appstore. For more information, see www.ricksteves.com/audioeurope. You can also follow me on Facebook and Twitter.

Additional Resources

Tourist Information: www.goscandinavia.com
Passports and Red Tape: www.travel.state.gov
Packing List: www.ricksteves.com/packing
Travel Insurance: www.ricksteves.com/insurance
Cheap Flights: www.kayak.com
Airplane Carry-on Restrictions: www.tsa.gov
Updates for This Book: www.ricksteves.com/update

How Was Your Trip?

If you'd like to share your tips, concerns, and discoveries after using this book, please fill out the survey at www.ricksteves.com/feedback. Thanks in advance—it helps a lot.

PRACTICALITIES

INDEX

Explore Europe

At ricksteves.com you can browse through thousands of articles, videos, photos and radio interviews, plus find a wealth of money-saving travel tips for planning your dream trip. And with our mobile-friendly website, you can easily access all this great travel information anywhere you go.

TV Shows

Preview the places you'll visit by watching entire half-hour episodes of Rick Steves' Europe (choose from all 100 shows) on-demand, for free.

your travel dreams into affordable reality

Radio Interviews

Enjoy ready access to Rick's vast library of radio interviews covering travel

tips and cultural insights that relate specifically to your Europe travel plans.

Travel Forums

Learn, ask, share! Our online community of savvy travelers is a great resource

for first-time travelers to Europe, as well as seasoned pros. You'll find forums on each country, plus travel tips and restaurant/hotel reviews. You can even ask one of our well-traveled staff to chime in with an opinion.

Travel News

Subscribe to our free Travel News e-newsletter, and get monthly updates from Rick on what's happening in Europe.

Audio Europe™

Rick's Free Travel App

Get your FREE **Rick Steves Audio Europe**™ app to enjoy...

- Dozens of self-guided tours of Europe's top museums, sights and historic walks
- Hundreds of tracks filled with cultural insights and sightseeing tips from Rick's radio interviews
- All organized into handy geographic playlists
- For iPhone, iPad, iPod Touch, Android

With Rick whispering in your ear, Europe gets even better.

Find out more at ricksteves.com

Experience maximum Europe

Save time and energy

This guidebook is your independent-travel toolkit. But for all it delivers, it's still up to you to devote the time and energy it takes to manage the preparation and logistics that are essential for a happy trip. If that's a hassle, there's a solution.

Rick Steves Tours

A Rick Steves tour takes you to Europe's most interesting places with great

with minimum stress

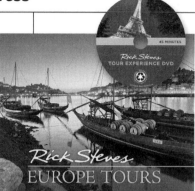

guides and small groups of 28 or less. We follow Rick's favorite itineraries, ride in comfy buses, stay in family-run hotels, and bring you intimately close to the Europe you've traveled so far to see. Most importantly, we take away the logistical headaches so you can focus on the fun.

Join the fun

This year we'll take 18,000 free-spirited travelers— nearly half of them repeat

customers—along with us on 40 different itineraries, from Ireland to Italy to Istanbul. Is a Rick Steves tour the right fit for your travel dreams? Find out at ricksteves.com, where you can also get Rick's latest tour catalog and free Tour Experience DVD.

Europe is best experienced with happy travel partners. We hope you can join us.

See our itineraries at ricksteves.com

EUROPE GUIDES

Best of Europe
Eastern Europe
Europe Through the Back Door
Mediterranean Cruise Ports
Northern European Cruise Ports

COUNTRY GUIDES

Croatia & Slovenia
England
France
Germany
Great Britain
Ireland
Italy
Portugal
Scandinavia
Spain
Switzerland

CITY & REGIONAL GUIDES

Amsterdam, Bruges & Brussels
Barcelona
Budapest
Florence & Tuscany
Greece: Athens & the Peloponnese
Istanbul
London
Paris
Prague & the Czech Republic
Provence & the French Riviera
Rome
Venice
Vienna, Salzburg & Tirol

SNAPSHOT GUIDES

Basque Country: Spain & France
Berlin
Bruges & Brussels
Copenhagen & the Best of
   Denmark
Dublin
Dubrovnik
Hill Towns of Central Italy
Italy's Cinque Terre
Krakow, Warsaw & Gdansk
Lisbon
Madrid & Toledo
Milan & the Italian Lakes District
Munich, Bavaria & Salzburg
Naples & the Amalfi Coast
Northern Ireland
Norway
Scotland
Sevilla, Granada & Southern Spain
Stockholm

POCKET GUIDES

Amsterdam
Athens
Barcelona
Florence
London
Paris
Rome
Venice

Rick Steves guidebooks are published by Avalon Travel,
a member of the Perseus Books Group.

NOW AVAILABLE:
eBOOKS, DVD & BLU-RAY

TRAVEL CULTURE

Europe 101
European Christmas
Postcards from Europe
Travel as a Political Act

eBOOKS

*Nearly all Rick Steves guides are
available as ebooks. Check with
your favorite bookseller.*

RICK STEVES' EUROPE DVDs

11 New Shows 2013–2014
Austria & the Alps
Eastern Europe
England & Wales
European Christmas
European Travel Skills & Specials
France
Germany, BeNeLux & More
Greece, Turkey & Portugal
Iran
Ireland & Scotland
Italy's Cities
Italy's Countryside
Scandinavia
Spain
Travel Extras

BLU-RAY

Celtic Charms
Eastern Europe Favorites
European Christmas
Italy Through the Back Door
Mediterranean Mosaic
Surprising Cities of Europe

PHRASE BOOKS & DICTIONARIES

French
French, Italian & German
German
Italian
Portuguese
Spanish

JOURNALS

Rick Steves Pocket Travel Journal
Rick Steves Travel Journal

PLANNING MAPS

Britain, Ireland & London
Europe
France & Paris
Germany, Austria & Switzerland
Ireland
Italy
Spain & Portugal

RickSteves.com **@RickSteves**

Rick Steves books and DVDs are available at bookstores
and through online booksellers.

Photo © Patricia Feaster

Avalon Travel
a member of the Perseus Books Group
1700 Fourth Street
Berkeley, CA 94710

Printed in Canada by Friesens.

ISBN 978-1-63121-061-7

For the latest on Rick's lectures, guidebooks, tours, public radio show, and public
television series, contact Rick Steves' Europe, 130 Fourth Avenue North, Edmonds,
WA 98020, 425/771-8303, www.ricksteves.com, rick@ricksteves.com.

Rick Steves' Europe
Managing Editor: Risa Laib
Editorial & Production Manager: Jennifer Madison Davis
Editors: Glenn Eriksen, Tom Griffin, Cameron Hewitt, Suzanne Kotz, Cathy Lu,
  Carrie Shepherd
Editorial & Production Assistant: Jessica Shaw
Editorial Intern: Stacie Larsen
Researchers: Glenn Eriksen, Cameron Hewitt
Maps & Graphics: David C. Hoerlein, Sandra Hundacker, Lauren Mills, Mary Rostad

Avalon Travel
Senior Editor & Series Manager: Madhu Prasher
Editor: Jamie Andrade
Associate Editor: Maggie Ryan
Copy Editor: Patrick Collins
Proofreader: Jennifer Malnick
Indexer: Beatrice Wikander
Production & Typesetting: Tabitha Lahr, Rue Flaherty
Cover Design: Kimberly Glyder Design
Maps & Graphics: Kat Bennett, Mike Morgenfeld

Photo Credits
Front Cover: Stockholm, Sweden © Sean Pavone/Dreamstime.com
Additional Photography: Dominic Arizona Bonuccelli, Tom Griffin, Sonja Groset,
  Cameron Hewitt, David C. Hoerlein, Lauren Mills, Moesgaard Museum, Rick
  Steves, Ian Watson, Chris Werner (photos are used by permission and are the
  property of the original copyright owners).

ABOUT THE AUTHOR

RICK STEVES

 Since 1973, Rick Steves has spent 100 days every year exploring Europe. Along with writing and researching a bestselling series of guidebooks, Rick produces a public television series *(Rick Steves' Europe),* a public radio show *(Travel with Rick Steves),* and an app and podcast *(Rick Steves Audio Europe);* writes a nationally syndicated newspaper column; organizes guided tours that take over 20,000 travelers to Europe annually; and offers an information-packed website (www.ricksteves.com). With the help of his hardworking staff of 100 at Europe Through the Back Door—in Edmonds, Washington, just north of Seattle—Rick's mission is to make European travel fun, affordable, and culturally enlightening for Americans.

Connect with Rick:

 facebook.com/RickSteves   twitter: @RickSteves

More for your trip!
Maximize the experience with Rick Steves as your guide

Guidebooks
Dozens of European city and country guidebooks

Planning Maps
Use the map that's in sync with your guidebook

Rick's TV Shows
Preview where you're going with 6 shows on Scandinavia

Free! Rick's Audio Europe™ App
Hear Scandinavia travel tips from Rick's radio shows

Small Group Tours
Take a lively Rick Steves tour through Scandinavia

For all the details, visit ricksteves.com